A Journey
Toward
Awakening

Craig Bergland

DEDICATION

For Erin, who taught me what real love is and who has stood by my side through thick and thin. It is she who holds open the space in which my life has evolved and in which our love continues to grow.

CONTENTS

ACKNOWLEDGMENTS

Writing this book has been an exciting journey for many reasons. One is that I have grown and transformed over the past fifteen years more than I would every have dreamed possible, and my hope is that in sharing some of my story with you that you will realize that anything is possible. Spirituality does not have to be an abstract exercise in wasting time, but instead can truly transform your life. The key is not to be confined by the traditions but rather to reach beyond them until you find your truth.

I have been influenced by so many authors and spiritual teachers, especially my spiritual director Pat Zealley, Thomas Merton, Richard Rohr, Domo Geshe Rinpoche, Bishop John Shelby Spong, Thich Nhat Hanh, Sharon Salzberg, Pema Chodron, Tara Brach, Jack Kornfield, Noah Levine, Stephen and Ondrea Levine, and His Holiness the 14th Dalai Lama. I have been encouraged in the writing of this book by my colleagues in The Universal Anglican Church, the denomination of which I am the Founding and

Presiding Bishop. I am privileged to serve with the finest group of people I have ever met. We are a voluntary association, unlike institutional Churches, and also bi-vocational clergy. In other words, our clergy stay because they believe in the work we do, not because they need a paycheck or health insurance. In the early days of our Church, I had no idea how blessed I would be by the clergy who would share our vision. I am honored and humbled to call them my friends.

I have been encouraged in the writing of this book and in countless other ways by my friend and brother from another mother, Bishop John L. Selders, Jr.. We met because we had both approached the same woman to carve our crosier, or bishop's staff. After speaking with both of us, she told each of us that we needed to get to know one another because of how much we seemed to have in common. It was a prophetic recommendation! When John and I first met we discovered that we had so much more in common that the very obvious fact that we are *outstandingly* handsome men. We both were raised in the Midwest and carry with us Midwestern sensibilities. We have different ethnicities and come from different spiritual backgrounds - but our journeys share many points of convergence and we share common perspectives to an almost frightening degree. John is a tremendously talented musician and singer, and I wish I was. John has opened doors for this ministry countless times, as well as for me personally, and is indeed closer to me than a brother. I pray that each of you find a friend like the friend I have found in John. We each know that if we call and say that we need help it will be given without question.

I am indebted as well to my colleague in ministry here in Milwaukee, The Rt. Rev. (Bishop) Jeffrey Montoya. It is a joy to work with someone you truly like and who is not afraid to speak the truth. It was he, in a particularly cantankerous mood one day as we shared lunch, who responded to my statement that I felt as if I needed to do a major rewrite to this book, "Bishop, you can rewrite forever and never publish the book. Just finish it!" He was, as usual, correct – but I did the rewrite anyway! Like all good leaders from different yet similar backgrounds, we sometimes clash but always from a place of integrity and with the desire for what is best. Bishop Jeffrey is a decade and a half younger than I, and I recognize that in him I sometimes see myself those many years ago and respond more to who I was than who he is. For that I beg his ongoing forgiveness and patience.

Last but most definitely not least I am indebted not only for her support in the writing of this book but also for transforming my life, to my wife Erin. In our time together my greatest false belief about myself was that I was unlovable on some level and nobody would stay with me should I prove to be flawed and human has been healed. Erin has loved me despite my humanity and my profound flaws. In doing so she has taught me what true love is, has been a support in everything I have attempted, and has nursed me back to health after three significant surgeries in the twelve plus years we have been together. I have often said to her that I am very glad there isn't a lemon law for husbands, or she certainly could have returned me as a defective model! We were together not even a year when both my children were diagnosed with bipolar disorder. Many a lesser woman would have walked away, and I could not have blamed her if she had, but she has stood by my side every minute of every day. I am blessed beyond belief by her love, support, intelligence, beauty, and presence in my life, and pray that I can be the husband she so richly deserves.

This story is not over. I harbor no delusions about being fully awakened, but then again the path **is** the goal!

Peace, Blessings, and All Good!

+cb

1 THE BEGINNING

There was a scene in the Steve Martin movie <u>The</u> <u>Jerk</u> that made me uncomfortable. I have since learned that discomfort is a sure sign that I need to explore something further. The scene was the opening scene wherein Steve Martin's character says, "I was born a poor black child," as the camera pans the width of the foot of a king size bed with several pair of small black feet sticking out from under the covers and moving left and right to the beat of a song being played. Finally the camera gets to a pair of white feet with no rhythm at all, moving in random directions completely unrelated to either each other or the music. Like the character in the movie, I always felt somehow different, somehow out of place, and that feeling – unbeknownst to me at the time – was, like Steve Martin's character, related to my family of origin.

I was born a middle class white child in 1960 about five weeks before John F. Kennedy was elected President. For those too young to remember, the middle class was something most people aspired to and included a house in the suburbs with a two car garage and two and one half children. The women in these middle class families stayed home and worked tirelessly and largely unrecognized as housewives. The men most often worked in offices in places called "factories," which actually made things called "products," and they tended to oversee production or design of the things the company made or else sold them to distributors. Many of the jobs were called "middle management," and the people who inhabited them were often called "junior executives," both of which became extinct during the early 1990s. During my first year of life we lived in a duplex on the south side of Milwaukee, eventually moving into an "experimental California subdivision," also on the south side of Milwaukee. We lived there until I was six. I don't remember much about those years, but I remember a few things.

The so-called California Subdivision probably had no relationship to anything in California. I have watched many, many police shows based in Los

Angeles and set during that period, and I never saw Adam-12 or Joe Friday drive down a city neighborhood with no curbs, storm drains in the middle of the street, and the streets sloped toward the middle. All of the sidewalks ran between the back yards of properties. Perhaps they were looking forward to the day when mugging became a popular career field and trying to provide muggers with a safe haven from which to pounce on their prey unobserved by patrol cars. It was, to be sure, an innocent time for the culture if not so much for me.

I do remember playing with a little girl down the street whose name I don't recall but who was rather bossy. I recall thinking she most resembled Lucy Van Pelt from *Peanuts*. Her favorite pastime was to tip the sand-filled awning that provided shade over my sandbox at just the right moment to pour sand into my unsuspecting eyes. Much like Charlie Brown, who kept trying to kick that damn football Lucy held, for some reason I kept playing in the sandbox with my Lucy longer than any reasonable person should have.

A kid named George lived across the street. We

were not allowed to cross the street because we surely would have been killed by traffic had we tried. Never mind that our neighborhood was a maze of alleys masquerading as profoundly winding streets and so every intersection was a massive collection of speed bumps as street-alleys converged and so it was impossible to maintain a speed of over ten miles per hour, venturing into the street was sure to bring death at the hands, or bumper, of a car defying the laws of physics and flying at sixty miles per hour through our ill-conceived California subdivision. Anyway, George lived across the street and had a pogo stick. A pogo stick, if you don't remember, was a stick that most resembled an Orthodox Cross with all the arms parallel to the ground. The lower arm served as a foot rest, one on each side of the center bar, while the upper arm was where the pogo stick rider held on for dear life. Inside the contraption was a massive spring, so when you jumped up and down on your pogo stick it bounced, creating endless fun for the easily amused. Back in the 1960s, of course, everything was metal and no child wore a helmet for any reason, except the epileptics who wore leather football helmets without facemasks from the 1940s.

Well, George just loved his pogo stick. He would bounce on the driveway of his home across the demilitarized zone...I mean, the street, for hours on end. Apparently, his family didn't understand the concept of a California subdivision or they would have kept him in the back yard, safe and out of sight where children belong. Did I mention the pogo stick was metal? You see, George so loved his *metal* pogo stick that even rain and thunder couldn't keep him from bouncing up and down for hours on his driveway. Sometimes it would rain so hard he was just a blur from inside our front window, bouncing up and down in the prepubescent equivalent of orgasmic bliss. Thunder didn't stop George, either. He was oblivious to danger. His parents did at least bring him in from bouncing on his lightning rod after the first half dozen lightening strikes or so. It was a different time, to be sure. I have often wondered whether or not George survived his lightening rod phase.

Homes in this California subdivision were all

ranch homes with attached garages, and they all featured sliding interior doors to maximize space. This worked out quite well for me since apparently I was a bit anal retentive as a child for reasons that aren't clear to me now. When my ability to retain my bowel movements reached its limit I could simply step into the closet in my bedroom, slide the door shut, and give birth to a used car salesman in my underpants right there in the closet. I then stood very still in the closet, not wanting to disturb the newborn, until to my horror the door slid open from *the other side* and there stood my mother with a moderately disgusted look on her face – having no doubt just caught a whiff of the pungent aroma of the afterbirth which had up to that point been trapped in the closet.

I also remember having a stick horse, the kind with mop hair. Back then, because it was the 1960s, stick horses were made from broomsticks rather than plastic and we weren't afraid. I loved the show "Bonanza," and my favorite character was Adam. I had no use for Hoss, Little Joe, Wing Nut the Chinese cook, and certainly not "Paw". Even back then, decades before Brittney Spears, the white hair with black eyebrows thing was an issue for me. Adam, however, was cool, and he was also on "Have Gun, Will Travel," which was so much cooler than hanging around with pretty-boy Michael Landon – but, I digress. When Bonanza was about to start, I would wait on my stick horse down the hallway that led to the bedrooms waiting to be cued so that as Adam rode through the blazing map I would arrive in the living room. My father, however, got great glee from calling me Hoss or Little Joe. To my three or four year old mind this was serious business, indeed, and I would tolerate no joking around. Once, he called me "Batman." I grasped my stick horse by its stick body and hit him square in the nuts with the head of the horse, accomplishing the biological equivalent of driving a hanging curve ball deep into the second deck over the left field wall. Although I was not sure why he was writhing around on the floor in pain, I sensed my identity problem might be solved. In retrospect, my chosen target was probably not accidental.

Sometime in those years, I don't recall exactly when, my father had surgery for ankle spurs. Medical care being a bit more primitive in those days, he was off work for a while. I remember him using a wheelchair to get around the house, but I don't remember crutches – which does not mean he didn't use them, of course. I remember being uncomfortable that he was there, and even more uncomfortable when my mother left for the grocery store. Much later in life I would have flashbacks involving the kitchen floor in this home, and although I never saw the faces I know they were real. Today I couldn't even begin to tell you what that kitchen looked like although I do remember our boxer, Charlie, eating his dinner in that kitchen and being fascinated that his tail was up. I slid from my chair, exclaimed "hole!" and thrust my index finger inside Charlie, apparently concerned for his prostate health. It turned out to be an excellent laxative. I also later noticed Charlie's testicles as he stood on my parent's bed and thought I should check him for testicle cancer, which caused him to empty his bladder on my parent's bed. I was a veterinarian in the making! Outside of those experimental moments, the only rooms I remember in that house are my closet and the living room.

Just less than a year before we moved to the suburb of Wauwatosa – at that time sure proof of having attained middle class status – and two weeks before my fifth birthday, my brother Kurt was born. My only other memory from that house is of sitting on our gold sofa with my new baby brother on my lap, who to me seemed like an alien from outer space, while people took pictures. I don't mean to imply that most people have solid memories of their early years. In fact, the opposite is true for most people. The truth is that even in my early twenties most of my childhood through High School graduation was lost to me. I remember bits and pieces, a glimpse here and there, an anecdote every now and again. As time has passed, I have occasionally remembered another story, and have made peace with the reality that I don't remember much – and much of what I do remember is rather unpleasant.

2 MOVING ON UP

My father was raised in Bay View, a section of Milwaukee that today has become somewhat gentrified, somewhat a haven for artist and other creative types, and is actually a desirable place to live in the city. Back in my father's time, it was a haven for 1950s leather jacket and white T-shirt wearing greaser types. For fun in the wee hours of the morning my father and his friends would walk to the Dutchland Dairy restaurant on 6th and Oklahoma, rip a parking meter from the concrete sidewalk, and throw it through the front window. He also learned that if you put a can of Welch's Grape Juice in the sun shining through the basement window it would eventually turn to wine. Not good wine, of course, but wine with alcohol content that will get you intoxicated, which is all he cared about at the time – and, quite possibly, aside from work, the only thing that really mattered throughout the rest of his life. Clearly, his pain ran deep.

My paternal grandfather's family came to the United States from Norway via Canada, landing in the

Dakotas. My grandfather, Peter, was one of twelve siblings and the one who migrated furthest east to Milwaukee. Others ended up in California, the Pacific Northwest, Minnesota, and of course some stayed in North and South Dakota. If you stumble across a Bergland, they are most likely related to me in some way because the more common spelling is "Berglund," and those people are a dime a dozen wannabes. My paternal grandmother Ruth's family came from God only knows where prior to landing in Missouri. She was always very evasive about her roots including her ethnicity, which for that time in history was rather unusual. I've always wondered if that reflected a detachment from her family of origin which, given the few people from it we encountered, seemed to be filled with more than a little mental illness mixed with a fair amount of toothless banjo players who spent their time "a ways up off the river" waiting for strangers to arrive. Her family also included a fair number of traveling tent revival preachers and healers, the religious form of a toothless banjo player in those parts.

My father's relationship with my grandfather is

difficult to assess. His mother was a profoundly bad cook, elevating both over- and under-cooking to art forms. A story survives in family lore about the bread she used to make, which tended to be rather heavy and burnt. Allegedly my grandfather, who was a legendary High School football coach in Milwaukee as well as a history teacher and pastor, took my father out into their yard on Superior Street to play catch. The "football" was a loaf of my grandmother's burnt bread. When Ruth looked out the window there was hell to pay. My grandfather, whose idea the whole thing had been the first place, sent my father in to apologize. It was a foreshadowing of my father's relationship with my mother. My grandfather also wanted my father to be the Middle Linebacker on his football team. My father was big for the time, standing six feet three, and an ideal Middle Linebacker but he wanted to play the tuba in the marching band. After forcing my father to endure a number of practices getting the crap beat out of him, my grandfather finally allowed him to be in the marching band.

My paternal grandparents were people of strong

religious faith. They were Methodists, and my grandfather was the pastor of what today is Faith United Methodist Church in West Allis, Wisconsin during World War II. He was also a High School social studies teacher. They were people of modest means who believed in the tithe even if it meant there wasn't enough to go around at home. That created in my father an animosity toward denominations that resulted in our joining the independent First Congregational Church on moving to Wauwatosa in 1966. Apparently, he didn't mind giving but he did want his money to stay at home. My father was his parents' only child, having been born when his father was thirty-seven and his mother thirty-four, quite late in life for those times. When I was a teenager my mother used to tell me stories of my paternal grandmother not wanting children and having performed at-home abortions by running up and down the steps with a "mixing spoon in her crotch" to induce miscarriage. It's hard to decide what the worst part of that fiction is, the impropriety of the sharing, the abysmal misunderstanding of anatomy and reproduction, or the alcoholic fog that produced the fiction, but none of it is very pretty. In any event, they were older when I was born and we lived across town so I never felt very close to them, nor was I particularly inclined to touch their spoons! My paternal grandfather passed away in 1976, two years before my parents' separation and divorce. My paternal grandmother lived well into her eighties, often inviting me to come over to help her "sort her pennies." For some reason I never found that invitation extremely compelling. She was also one of those grandmothers who was physically imposing, tall for the time, wobbly on her high heels even in relative youth, and stood in the living room of our home gazing at herself in the large mirror over the fireplace while "smoothing" the material of her dress or, depending on your perspective, stroking her breasts. Invariably, that ritual was followed be the desire to kiss her grandchildren "on the lips" with a wet, sloppy, lipstick-laden kiss. It wasn't every day I got such an invitation, a fact for which I was eternally thankful, but it was an unavoidable offering every time she came around.

My strongest memory of my paternal

grandfather was that when he prayed at holiday meals he could go on forever. It was serious business. Everyone had to be seated at the table, and the food often got cold as he petitioned the Lord at some length. One September, at one of our birthday meals, he began his long-winded prayer. My brother and I had recently seen and were quite impressed with a television program about hippies for Jesus. In fact, we got in big trouble for spending a long time spinning in circles while on vacation chanting "I'm freaking out." At the time I was around thirteen years old, which would have made Kurt eight years old. At the end of the exhaustive and exhausting prayer, on top of the "Amen," my brother exclaimed, "Right on with Jesus!" There was a period of silence as we waited for the explosion. My grandfather must have evaluated Kurt's ejaculation as an authentic expression of Jesus-love (it wasn't) and so said, "Let's eat." Disaster averted, no thanks to those dirty hippies for Jesus.

My mother's parents, Reinhard and Winifred Schroeder, were very different from my father's parents. They were both native German speakers, my grandfather's family having escaped what was then Prussia in the days immediately before the start of World War I and my grandmother's family having come here a bit earlier. She never spoke much of coming to America. Her father was pastor of Tabor Church, a large church of the Evangelical United Brethren denomination, which today is part of the United Methodist Church. Nana was the church organist, which is how she met my grandfather. My grandfather was a working man, having dropped out of school to support his family. He worked his entire adult life at Cutler Hammer (later A.O. Smith) as a warehouse supervisor until his retirement in 1968. When we moved to Wauwatosa in 1966, we moved two blocks from my grandparents who had moved from the city of Milwaukee to the suburbs in 1940 and built one of the first homes on their block. It was really my grandparents who provided my first glimpse of unconditional love, and whenever I needed to retreat and talk I could ride my bike to their house.

Although she clearly loved her mother, my mother was ambivalent about her father and had almost nothing to do with her extended family, which also lived in the area but whom we rarely saw. The only time I really remember seeing them was for someone's graduation party at my Uncle Bill's house where they gave me Brandy on the rocks and I learned how insane Brandy drinkers really are. Uncle Bill was Grandpa Schroeder's brother and they had a third surviving brother at the time, Harry. The three of them could have passed for triplets. Years later, and only after years of therapy and dealing with my own abuse history, reflecting on something that happened when I was ten years old, did I understand why my mother was estranged from her extended family.

The summer between third and fourth grade my father converted my bicycle to a coveted sting-ray, complete with chopper handle bars and a red banana seat. I was now officially an almost ten year old bad ass. In his retirement, my grandpa had taken up bicycle riding and each summer he would tune up our bikes so they rode better than new. (Grandpa Schroeder had three copies of every tool Craftsman made.) One day he said that he wanted to take me for a bike ride to meet someone. I was thrilled! We would even be crossing Center Street! God only knew what lay on the other side of Center Street, but this much was certain: I had been forbidden to cross it. He told me it would be a bit of a long ride, and I was even more excited. In truth it was probably three or four miles, but to a nine year old that can be a marathon. We set out, and I was so proud to be going somewhere with grandpa. Not only did we cross Center Street, we crossed an even bigger street I hadn't even know existed – Burleigh Street! Sweet Jesus we had to be getting near the Promised Land! Then we were riding through some alleys, which evoked memories of the California subdivision, and we came to what I now understand to be a mobile home parked behind a small house just south of 92nd Street and Lisbon Avenue.

Inside the home was a man who could have been Colonel Sanders' twin brother, complete with shocking white hair and the perfect goatee for his doppelganger. My grandpa introduced me to my Great Uncle Connie with great pride. We went inside Connie's home, had something cool to drink, and grandpa and Connie visited. After a fashion we returned back, somehow once again surviving the crossing of both Burleigh and Center Streets, to my grandparent's home. Eventually, I returned home and my mother asked what I did that day. Not knowing better, I told her of our adventure across the demilitarized zone. She exploded. She ranted, she raved, and she called my grandpa on the telephone and told him if he ever did "that" again it would be the last time he saw any of us. Presumably, "that" was taking me or my brother to see Uncle Connie, but I had no idea why. Years later, after learning of the lasting impacts of abuse on those who do not seek treatment, I realize that Connie was most likely a profoundly unpleasant influence in my mother's childhood. In retrospect, there is no other reason she would have become so upset at her father taking me to meet his brother. Even crossing the demilitarized zone that was Center Street wouldn't have done it.

Not too long after this my father lost his job. He had worked for several years for a company called AC Spark Plug. While much of the company did indeed make spark plugs there was another division heavily involved in the defense industry and contracting with NASA to design the guidance system for Saturn V rockets – the rockets which carried the Mercury, Gemini, and Apollo space capsules into space. Although he never mentioned it, I am quite sure those same guidance systems powered missiles, including nukes. After all, a rocket is a rocket no matter its cargo. As 1970 approached, the space program as we had known it was winding down. The Space Shuttle was in the design stages, and the Milwaukee operations would close. The plant would continue as AC Delco and make automobile stereo systems but the guidance system and other military operations would move to Kentucky. Perhaps the memories of toothless banjo players in his family tree made Kentucky seem less than appealing, but more than likely it was my mother's steadfast refusal to move away from her parents, Uncle Connie and the other unseen family members notwithstanding, that led to his decision to stay here in the Milwaukee area.

During this time, in fact it may have started with

the move to Wauwatosa to further establish our middle class credentials; we began vacationing "up north." For those not from Wisconsin, up north refers to any location in the northern half of Wisconsin, although as a genuine up north traditionalist I believe you really have to be in the northern third of Wisconsin to have your trip qualify as an authentic up north trip. For our family it was the Three Lakes, Eagle River, Conover, and Minocqua. One of those years we landed in a place where, much to my surprise, a friend of mine from school appeared on the lake, coming around the corner in a rowboat with a small engine on it and driven by his father. They invited me back to their summer home on the same lake, and although I had never really done much with this friend during the school year I suppose people who vacation must be okay and so we all readily agreed I could go. For several days I did go, picked up and returned by my personal Wicked Uncle Gus, and what happened there made whatever happened on the kitchen floor of the California subdivision seem inconsequential. If there is one event that impacted my first thirty years of my life more, I don't know what it could possibly be. That having been said, I now realize that the most damaging experiences weren't these vacation experiences, but rather what would happen at the kitchen table during my junior high and high school years right there at our middle class Wauwatosa dinner table.

3 CADDYSHACK

My family, for all its pretensions to middle class status, had a heavy dose of blue collar roots with which my mother never really made peace. As I mentioned, my father grew up in a working class neighborhood on the south side of Milwaukee, a city that at that time was largely populated by hearty, working class German and Polish immigrants, with the odd Norwegian, Swede, Italian, Irishman, and God knows what else scattered about. It was a foundry town and a beer town, and in school the kids whose fathers worked at Pabst fought with the kids whose dads worked for Miller, or Schlitz, or Blatz just out of an odd sense of family pride. If you worked in the brewery you drank on the job for free, and took home beer at a greatly reduced price. If your friend's father worked for the brewery, his fridge was filled with "shorties," short filled bottles that were rejected in the quality control process and given to workers. The only city with more bars per capita than Milwaukee is Boston, and I can explain that with one word – Irishmen. We Germans, Poles, and Prussians love our beer, but for Irishmen of my grandparents' generation drinking seems to have been a vocation.

When my father left AC Spark Plug he worked for a short time for a small company near the railroad tracks in West Allis, not far from the Farmer's Market. I don't remember what the name of the company was or what they did, but I do remember he didn't stay there long because he was hoping for an offer from another company and that offer came through very quickly. He landed in the industry called "paper converting," where he would spend the rest of his working days. Paper converting equipment essentially takes paperboard and turns it into packaging for everything from your McDonald's French Fry box to the boxes for any household pharmacy or food product you can imagine. He started supervising the factory, a step down from his former position but a point of entry. The first thing he did was move his office into the shop space, reasoning that he needed the workers to feel he was a part of their team. He played on the shop team rather than the office team during the company picnic softball and football games. In short, he understood people who "worked for a living" because those were his roots - and they loved him for it. Even as he was repeatedly promoted he kept a close working relationship with the people who really made his company successful, the shop people.

For reasons that aren't clear to me, as my father was transitioning into a new career, my mother was unraveling psychologically. When he started traveling for work, it got even worse. She read an article about botulism and from that moment forward everything had botulism. Never mind that botulism only occurs in canned goods and with modern packaging standards is extremely rare, in my mother's world botulism lurked around every corner. Anything that was vacuum packed or bottled, and eventually even those barriers to her phobia fell, was suspect. During those years I believe we threw away more food than we consumed. She also developed Obsessive-Compulsive features, having to return home several times when trying to leave for fear she hadn't turned off a burner or the oven – even if she hadn't used it that day.

The summer after my fourth grade year my

brother and I weren't allowed to leave our back yard because of a Chicken Pox pandemic. There is no record of such a pandemic in Milwaukee's history. I remember being just terrified at the notion of even venturing close to the white picket fence that surrounded our backyard for fear I would be infected by this horrible, albeit fictional, pandemic. To be sure, her anxiety permeated our lives. It was mixed with a blend of narcissism and paranoia for good measure. When she backed out of the driveway one day and hit the neighbor's yard waste cans that were sitting in *their* driveway, she complained they had placed them there just so she would hit them. When she finally agreed to see a therapist, it lasted one visit. He sent her home with a relaxation tape to address her obsession with botulism, but in her mind he was trying to get her to kill her family.

My parents' drinking also took an upswing during these years. One of my few memories from the early Wauwatosa period involves our purchase of a new refrigerator. I know it was the early years, because my father was drinking Weber beer. Weber was manufactured just outside Milwaukee in Waukesha (the

Wisconsin home of toothless banjo players back in the day) and you could buy a case for two dollars and change. I have no idea why I remember that, but I do. As the family income increased, he moved up to a better class of swill, but back in the day it was Weber that my father had stocked in the brand new kitchen fridge. Mind you the older fridge was in the basement to serve as the beer and soda fridge but for some reason my father, perhaps celebrating the new fridge or perhaps anticipating being unable to descend the basement steps safely in a few hours, had every bottle from the case in the brand new kitchen fridge when his parents (abstinent Methodists from whom my parents attempted to hide the fact that they drank) arrived to examine the new appliance. Oblivious to my father's bar-back project, my mother flung open the fridge and exclaimed "Just look at how much room there is inside!" revealing twenty-four chilling brown bottles of Weber beer. Immediately flinging the door shut in a classic example of closing the barn door after the beer has escaped, the subject was changed. I remember my parents later discussing whether or not his parents had "noticed" the beer. Noticed? A nearly empty refrigerator, all of the other food having been moved to the basement fridge so that it wouldn't spoil while the new one cooled down, with a case of beer in it? Even at my young age I was sure our family prohibition officers had missed it completely...

My parents drinking increased until by about eighth grade I was their primary bartender. My specialty was Manhattans, Martinis, and Bloody Maries – always doubles, but since my parents' single was a double, these were all quadruples. Cocktails before dinner, followed by either beer or more cocktails with dinner, and topped off with a fifth of bourbon after dinner was a pretty standard night. At least I didn't have to pour the bourbon – they kept that bottle under the kitchen sink. I was the beer and mixed drink runner, however.

Right around the bicentennial my father decided to start his own business, which lasted three years and then closed. To further cement our business owning, middle class status we joined a Country Club because my father loved playing golf. As I mentioned, my father grew up in a blue-collar environment that most resembled a James Dean movie. Although possessed of high IQ he wasn't much for nonsense, so his walking into Tuckaway Country Club was not unlike Al Czervik walking into Bushwood Country Club in the movie Caddyshack. That movie will probably always be my favorite movie, largely because I lived with Al Czervik – not quite as funny as Rodney Dangerfield, and completely oblivious to his status as Al Czervik's stand in, but Al nevertheless. To an already self conscious adolescent, it was beyond embarrassing. As an adult I can look back and appreciate that some of his behavior was quite intentional, like when he told another member of the club who was way too impressed with whichever pro golfer had used his locker during the Greater Milwaukee Open that he was just fine with Chi Chi Rodriguez (whose name he intentionally mispronounced as "Chai Chai Rot-wi-geeze") using his locker, "whoever that is."

Running behind all of these outward, carefully crafted middle class appearances was a hugely dysfunctional home life. My parents would begin drinking themselves into oblivion immediately upon arriving home in the evening. The more my father drank, the more passive he became. The more my mother drank, the more angry and abusive she became. In fact, every night as dinner ended my brother and I played an unspoken but nevertheless high-stakes game of can-we-get-away-before-the-rage-brakes-out. All of us spent untold hours as the target of her drunken rage, which most often involved repeating the same phrase over and over. They always began with "Do you know what your problem is?" but for some reason the answer was never that my problem was that I was stuck sitting at the table with two drunken fools. Her answer of choice for me was that I was "nothing but a goddamn adolescent." Sometimes she would abbreviate the mantra, most likely because she was too intoxicated to remember it, and just sneer "adolescent!" over and over. Being a pretty bright guy and aware of my age, I couldn't really deny that I was an adolescent. Nor could I understand what the problem was with being an adolescent, but apparently there was one.

Other times, she chose my father as the target

and we could eventually slip away from the table, but you had to be careful because if you attempted to leave too soon you could easily become the target of her venom. Whenever she tried to focus on my brother, I would attempt to shift her attention onto me with varying degrees of success. When my brother and I were eventually released from the table, her attention and rage always turned to my father. He was a "failure," "no good," "no businessman," "a harelip" and a host of other things I have either forgotten or blocked from my memory. Occasionally, I would have to go downstairs around three in the morning and ask them to be quiet because we had school the next day and needed to sleep. They would most often comply, but the next night my intervention was yet another piece of evidence that I was just a goddamn adolescent. The memory of my sexual abuse was hidden under a veil of repression that would not lift until I was thirty, but the daily verbal abuse took its toll on me and I never forgot it. It couldn't be repressed because it never stopped. My father began traveling more and more for work, which of course made for one less target at the dinner table.

There were other things, too. Our lives were micro-managed. We could never close our bedroom doors all the way no matter the reason. It was absolutely unacceptable to show pain whether physical or emotional. Everywhere you went, everything you did, every second of every minute of every day had to be accounted for. We were timed in the bathroom for fear we might be masturbating, which made my hobby of reading on the throne very difficult. It wasn't that I didn't masturbate, all teenage boys do. Marie Osmond in that Tiger Beat Magazine took my virginity and she hasn't called once since, the bitch. I didn't masturbate while using the bathroom. Can we say "ambiance," for crying out loud? I preferred to be alone in my room with Marie.

I desperately wanted to play football in Junior High, but my mother was certain I would be killed or rendered a paraplegic and wouldn't allow it. There was no going to friends' houses until high school, and then only friends who had been vetted. In retrospect, all of my high school friends came from families more or less as dysfunctional up as mine. On some sub-conscious level we must have recognized that we all were in the same boat and so none of us would think any of our parents were odd. Instinctively we all knew better than to invite a kid from a normal family to our home, even as we didn't realize our homes were abnormal. During high school my father decided I might be gay because I didn't bring any girls around, not recognizing that to bring a girl around a house of drunken chaos would surely have been social suicide!

4 THE CHURCH

Surely our involvement in the church rescued us from all of this, right? Well, no, not really. In fact, in many ways Church only made it worse. To understand the story you need to know that the official religion of the State of Wisconsin is not Christianity, Judaism, Buddhism, Hinduism, nor any of the other many wonderful world religions we might have chosen. The State Religion is the Green Bay Packers. If you want to go shopping on Sunday in Wisconsin and don't want to wait in long lines you go during the Packers' game. Of course in doing so you prove you are a godless heretic, but everything comes at a price. When I was a child in the California subdivision home I watched every Packers game with a green felt "31" pinned to the back of my T-shirt in honor of Packers' fullback Jim Taylor.

Now my parents were Green Bay Packer Christians. That meant that while they still conformed to the middle class notion that it was a good thing to belong to Church they also recognized that God much preferred them to worship in front of the Green Bay Packers game. The compromise was that First Congregational had an eleven o'clock service they would drop my brother and me off at church (a mixed message if ever there was one) and then my mother would return to pick us up at the first commercial break following the opening kickoff. It never lasted long into the season, probably only until my mother missed the first exciting play that happened in her absence.

So, although I had been periodically involved at church while growing up (actually Sunday school, since children were not welcome in actual worship) it probably won't surprise you to learn that I didn't have much use for it. There were many things that contributed to my dissatisfaction, among them terribly boring Sunday school classes that had as their primary focus Old Testament stories and outmoded technologies even for that time like felt boards, for crying out loud; the fact that my parents seldom attended and as most rescuers from toxic families do I was anxious about what would happen in my absence; the fact that the youth pastor and I didn't get along at all, he having made it clear that he didn't like kids who weren't present every week; and the cliques that had formed among the kids who were regular attendees. These little bastards, er, Christians, were among the *least* popular kids at school because they were such social misfits, but had managed to kiss the youth pastor and Sunday School teachers' asses enough to gain power in the pecking order of Sunday School life. So, as if it wasn't bad enough that I was only an average athlete and was pretty quiet at school because of the chaos at home and therefore took crap at school, here at church I was taking crap from those below me in the social pecking order at school! Oh, heavens yes, sign me up for more of that! Worse yet, these little nerds just loved to go camping. I had absolutely no interest being stuck in the woods with a know-it-all loudmouth girl and a boy with a peach fuzz mustache that looked for all the world like he had been sloppy eating a fudgsickle and whose voice had changed in the first grade.

As if my animosity around the Church wasn't bad enough during grade school and junior high, during high school we were required to attend two years of

Confirmation classes. The first year had as its focus the same damn Old Testament stories I had suffered through repeatedly during my periodic attendance at Sunday school. Yeah, yeah, Daniel and the lion's den and David and Goliath. Were these Church people on drugs? The only decent thing about the classes was that they were held every Thursday night right after school and the church was only three blocks from school, effectively delaying my return home for a couple of hours. Though the second year had a slightly more interesting focus, the New Testament, but the classes began at 9am on Saturday mornings, for God's sake! I don't know who came up with the brilliant idea of waking fifteen and sixteen year olds up early on Saturday morning to get them to love Jesus, but whoever they were they were certifiable idiots. Walking the three blocks to church after school on Thursday nights wasn't really a big deal. Walking a mile and a half at eight-thirty on Saturday morning to arrive by nine o'clock was a very big deal indeed. What's more, there were tests and quizzes throughout the two years! Wasn't there enough of that crap in real school? I wondered if all God cared about was how I scored on a test, given that he didn't seem to be showing up very much at home and at church seemed determined to get me to go camping. Since I was a good student the problem for me wasn't passing the tests (especially since I wrote cheat notes on the rubber soles of my chukka boots) but rather that spirituality had been reduced to academics.

During our senior year in high school, as graduation approached, we were required to meet with our Senior Pastor. He asked me what I wanted to do with my life. I answered honestly and said that I really didn't know, but I did know that I wanted to help other people. He then asked me the question I least expected, "Have you ever considered the ministry?" Without warning I exploded in laughter, spewing saliva into the air and onto his desk. I made a quick recovery, though, and said that I really didn't think that was for me. I am sure that smoothed everything over after I had exploded in disbelief, spittle, and hilarity at the thought of entering the vocation that was *his* life's calling. In retrospect, maybe he saw something I didn't.

I would like to tell you that I went away to college, but I didn't. It was out of the question. My mother wouldn't allow it. During the summer after my graduation I worked in the summer playground program in our local school district, drank a lot of beer, and played in the garage band I had played in throughout High School. Good God, we were awful. My father was working in New Jersey at the time and only returning home every other weekend. It was that summer my father came home and announced that he was leaving. I called him a selfish bastard, mostly because he was leaving me with the crazy drunken woman, and he said he would reconsider. He had been an absent father throughout high school, not really knowing who I was or understanding what I did, so it wasn't like his being gone was going to matter much. I suspect that I knew that the cross-generational bonding between my mother and I was only going to intensify, and it did. I was the one who had to call for child support when he was late and do many of the other tasks she should have taken on herself.

He came back into town on my 18th birthday,

September 28, 1978, and told me he was leaving for good. He said that the thing in his life he wouldn't trade anything for was all the traveling he had done and all the people he had met. I asked if he really meant that was more important to him than his kids, he said yes. He said we could sell his boat and use it for my tuition, but when it sold my mother kept the money. That was a large factor in my dropping out after two and one half years. Lacking both direction and money, there wasn't much point in going on.

Ironically, during my first years of college I tried to draw close to Church. I joined the church softball team and faithfully sat in the balcony at church most Sundays and on the bench most Tuesday nights. Then one night I was sitting on the bench and the youth pastor came from the stands, sat next to me on the bench, and told me that some people were upset because they were at church every Sunday but never getting into the games while people who never came to church were playing. I was shy, not given to question authority, but also very angry. I told him to count me among them, and walked away from church for what I honestly believed was the last time. Little did I know that I would be back in church in four years.

In the meantime, after dropping out of school and spending about six months working in a convenience store and getting held up by a man with a snub nose .38 pistol I decided this was not a viable long term employment solution. It was 1981, and the economy was terrible. I had no marketable skills, so I decided to enlist in the Air Force Reserves and go to electronics school. Needless to say, my mother went ballistic. The Air Force was even more dangerous than junior high School football. They were going to kill me and hide the body. She enlisted my uncle, who had been in the Army and stationed in Georgia during the Korean conflict, to ambush me at a dinner at his house just before departure to basic. In fairness, my uncle was a good man who didn't know what to do with my mother's histrionics. He told me there would be live fire exercises in the Air Force just like there were in the Marines. He told me I could be killed. In all honesty, that didn't seem like a really bad outcome to me, but I also knew it wasn't true.

Somehow I survived basic training in San Antonio, Texas from the beginning of July until the middle of August. I had never experienced heat and humidity like that in all my twenty years of life. Nobody ever fired a shot at me or anyone else. The worst part of it was the day we were assigned to duty cleaning up the base. I was assigned to ride with someone in the back of a large box van that drove around to all of the enlisted and officers' clubs to pick up bags of empty, but not rinsed, beer cans that would be recycled and the money used for various improvement projects around the base. I must say that the Air Force was ahead of the times in recycling. That having been said, there is little more nauseating than spending your day in the back of an unconditioned cargo van filled with stale, empty beer cans warmed to a temperature the exceeded one hundred degrees. Aromatherapy it wasn't.

Several of the guys had a hard time adjusting because Air Force basic is a big mind game, but having grown up in my family I knew just what to do and how to play the game. I told the other guys they had to understand that the drill instructors got to play with our minds for six weeks, but we knew that if we did what we were supposed to do we were walking out of there at the end of six weeks and nothing could stop us. How ironic was it that my abuse history actually prepared me for basic training? I later came to understand that what they were trying to do – break our wills so we would obey without question – had already been accomplished in my case at home. To me, these red-faced, screaming, drill sergeants were rank amateurs. In fact, I liked them.

The second time I had work duty, about two thirds of the way through basic, I was assigned to help a drill sergeant who was going to get a new crop of recruits in a couple of days. He spoke to me as if I was a human being, said please and thank you when giving me tasks, and explained to me that throughout the day he would be spending time getting himself in the right frame of mind for what he had to do over the next six weeks. I would see him looking at himself in a full length mirror, doing what I recognized from sports as "putting on a game face." I had been right! It *was* a game! The sad truth is that the outcome of this game, in every branch of the military, has a profoundly negative consequence on the people who don't see through it and consequently buy into the military. I have come to the conclusion that the more unsatisfactory the environment in which you grew up the more likely it is you will buy in. If you want to know how a human being can pull the trigger on another human being, all you have to look at is the reality that the military programs them to do so by stripping them of their identity and will to resist conformity. Later, when they are done with the people they have trained, they release them into society without benefit of re-programming them, although I am not sure complete re-programming is possible.

Just as I predicted, six weeks later I left for Chanute Air Force Base in Rantool, IL where I trained in Avionics. I learned basic electronics, and when I got out I ate up every electronics book I could find. By October 1982 I was living in Rockford, IL and working for Johnson & Johnson Ultrasound as a Field Service Engineer. My mother told me I was nothing but a no good, factory working "grunt" – her preferred term of derision for factory workers. By then I didn't care what she thought, I had done what nobody – including me –

thought I would be able to do. I was in a bit over my head, but I knew I would make it. I was officially a Yuppie, wearing jacket and tie to work every day.

5 RE-ENTRY

When I was twenty-three years old Grandpa Schroeder passed away suddenly while mowing the lawn. It came as quite a shock to me and I returned home to Milwaukee from my home in Rockford, Illinois immediately. As I watched my aunt and uncle's United Methodist Pastor work with my very dysfunctional family, I had an epiphany about ministry. Prior to that experience, I believed that all clergy did was to preach on Sundays and officiate at weddings, funerals, and Baptisms. If they were youth pastors, their job was to piss me off. Something changed a bit during my two and one half years at Marquette University. My first religion class was taught by Fr. Richard R. Roach. Prior to becoming a priest, Fr. Roach had been a fighter bomber pilot in the Royal Canadian Air Force. He told us about the day he flew his plane through the clouds and say the sun on the horizon - and realized he was there to destroy the beautify creation he was seeing so clearly that morning. He landed his aircraft, resigned his commission, and entered seminary. It was the first time I have been exposed to the idea of spirituality leading to a significant life change, and his story changed me. From that time forward, the only courses that meant anything to me were Theology and Philosophy courses. My problem was that I couldn't imagine doing anything with either of those subjects that would lead to gainful employment. Then there was that whole celibacy issue among Catholic priests, which had slightly less appeal than being dragged naked across broken glass for three miles by a team of horses and dropped into a salt bath. Marie Osmond had already gotten to me, and I wasn't going back.

Against this background, I encountered the United Methodist Pastor who displayed supreme skill in working with my family. His sensitivity, his knowledge, and his compassion were exceptional, and I got my first look at a pastor who was more than one dimensional. Something even more shocking began to happen. A still, small voice within started saying that this was what I was called to do. This wasn't exactly a message I was eager to hear! I still had a lot of misperceptions about clergy, but more than that I had a successful career underway as a field service engineer. That job required occasional overnight travel and I couldn't really control what time I returned home at night even when I wasn't traveling. These things were happening before colleges and universities started accommodating working students with Saturday and accelerated classes. I needed to go back to school to finish my degree, it seemed like a dream that was impossible to fulfill. I was a 1980s yuppie who didn't have a church relationship. What I knew with certainty was that, given my childhood, I wasn't eager to seek out the local Congregational Church! Before much time had passed, my job had transferred me to New England, and so my church search began anew.

My first stop in the Newburyport, Massachusetts area was a little Methodist church in a white, wooden building. About a week before visiting this church, a co-worker had told me a joke about a traveling tent revival preacher. Given my family history, I was all ears. The preacher set up shop, or tent, on the outskirts of town and posted handbills to let everyone know he was having a meeting that weekend. When the night came, the tent was packed. He manipulated the crowd with expertise through his choice of music and message, and then invited anyone in need of healing to come forward. Two men came forward, one walking on crutches and the other with no apparent physical issues. The preacher asked the first man, "What's your name, son, and what ails you?"

He replied, "My name is Fred, and I have been unable to walk without crutches since birth."

"Do you believe in Jesus?" came the question, and Fred assented. The preacher then said, "Go behind the curtain and be healed!" and Fred moved behind a temporary, seven foot high curtain that had been placed on the platform. The next gentleman approached, and the preacher asked, "What's your name, son, and what ails you?"

"B-B-B-B-B-Bob, and I sta-sta-sta-sta-stutter."

"Do you believe in Jesus?" came the question, and Bob nodded his head with vigor. The preacher then said, "Go behind the curtain and be healed!" and Bob moved behind the same curtain on the platform. With great passion and fervor, the preacher whipped the crowd into a frenzy. He invoked the Holy Spirit and shouted, "Fred, throw out your crutches!" and Fred's crutches came sailing over the top of the curtain. The pastor demanded, "Bob, speak to us!" and the reply came:

"F-F-F-F-Fred fell down!"

It was against this background that I entered the little Methodist church. It was a bi-level affair with the sanctuary on the upper floor and the offices and classrooms on the lower. At the entrance to the worship space stood an usher who must have been three hundred years old, because that's the law in most Christian churches – you prop the oldest guy in the world at the door so that the paramedics don't have to walk very far to find him when he collapses. We'll call the usher "Methuselah." I noticed that the hymn board had been converted to an attendance board and that the congregation usually numbered in the low teens. Upon examining the bulletin I learned that this church was served by a pastor who served several Methodist churches in the area and that day's worship would be led by what the Methodists call a lay liturgist.

As the first chords of the opening hymn were struck I heard a very loud telephone ringing in the lower level. As the first person in the procession entered the sanctuary, Methuselah began the treacherous descent down several steps to the lower lever, moving with the agility that befit his youth. As the procession continued to enter and the phone continued to ring, I noticed the man who was the lay liturgist and behind him an attractive young woman walking with the kind of metal crutches that indicated a long term problem with her legs. As she drew near the altar, the phone stopped ringing and, unbeknownst to us, Methuselah began his lightening fast (relatively speaking) return to the sanctuary with terrible news. The lay liturgist had just finished the call to worship when Methuselah burst (well, stumbled) into the sanctuary and exclaimed, "The Wilson's house just burned down!" The woman sitting in front of me reached into her purse, extracted a nitroglycerin tablet, and slipped it under her tongue. Throughout the sanctuary the massive gathering of twelve (Methuselah had updated the attendance board) gasped, screamed, or fought back tears as befit their relationship with the Wilson family. Fully expecting the lay liturgist to ask if everyone got out of the home safely and lead the congregation in prayer for the victims of this tragedy, I was more than a little shocked when he simply called for the first reading to be read. Clearly, this would not be my church home.

When it came time for the sermon the young woman with the crutches walked toward the pulpit, ascended its one step and stood at the beautiful, wooden pulpit. She preached a painfully predictable sermon, which was really more of a testimony based on that God-awful "Footprints" poem and how her life paralleled that poem than a sermon. That having been said, given that she was not a professional speaker or preacher, she acquitted her self adequately. When she finished, she stepped back from the pulpit, apparently forgetting about the one step she had ascended to get to the pulpit, fell backwards as her crutches sailed into the air, and a little voice in my head said "F-F-F-F-Fred fell down!"

I was laughing uncontrollably, but managing to stifle the sound. My shoulders, however, were betraying my glee. The lay liturgist did, thankfully, have the presence of mind to check that she was okay, helped her get her crutches under her and helped her back to her seat. I continued to laugh, now with even more intensity since I knew she was safe, and that damn voice in my head kept shouting "F-F-F-F-Fred fell down!" over and over. The next thing I knew it was the closing hymn and the altar party was headed back down the aisle where I just knew I was going to have to greet her and compliment her on her message without laughing in her face. Needless to say, I was the last person to leave the sanctuary and it was only by grace I kept my composure until in the car.

The next Sunday I decided to try something called the Episcopal Church about which I knew next to nothing. In fact, my only prior experience with Communion was in the Congregational Church. During our second year of Confirmation class – on Saturday mornings – they apparently decided it wasn't enough to wake us up early on Saturday morning, but we also had to drag our tired asses to Church on Sunday morning. We were instructed to sit in the balcony where our attendance would be taken, but nobody ever took our attendance. It was quite clear they didn't want us to sit with the "real members." Being there regularly meant that I was there once for Communion, which only happed a few times a year in that church. Now, I attended the 11am service because it afforded me the most sleep. I would set my alarm as late as I could and still make it to the cheap seats on time, which meant I usually didn't eat breakfast.

As the passed the tray of Wonder Bread dicc, I took one and began salivating immediately. Then we had to wait for the juice shot glasses to make it to the balcony and for the ushers to return the trays to their resting place. By now I was one of Pavlov's dogs, wishing there was a suction tube available so I would stop drooling on myself over a morsel of bread. Finally, the pastor said, "take, eat," and I raised my hand to my mouth and popped that bread into my mouth. Or did I? It dissolved so quickly in the ocean of saliva I was sure I had missed my mouth! I started looking around out of pure hunger rather than any sense of reverence. Then I heard an instruction to drink so I did my shot of grape juice while still searching for the Body of Christ between the theater seating in the balcony. Eventually, I decided I couldn't have missed my mouth but rather that white-bread Jesus wasn't very filling.

It was against this background that I entered St. Paul's Episcopal Church in Newburyport. Everything that would happen during worship was printed in the Book of Common Prayer or the hymnal. Given my recent experience as well as my abuse history, I found ritual to be very comforting. Best of all, Communion wasn't the irreverent experience I had encountered in the balcony of First Congregational. We approached the altar rail, knelt, and received the Sacrament in a reverent, worshipful way. I was hooked, and I had found my home. I enrolled in the Adult Confirmation Class and became an Episcopalian in 1984

While I found the Episcopal Church not too long after moving to Massachusetts, it would be seven more years before I finally returned home to Milwaukee to return to school to pursue my calling. In the meantime,

I had moved from New England, back to Milwaukee, and on to Indianapolis. All of the moves were related to work. My two children were born, and my marriage fell apart when their mother was diagnosed with bi-polar disorder. I was forced to confront my abuse history when I started dating someone who had herself been abused. Finally, I came to the undeniable conclusion that all of my attempts to micro-manage my life had failed.

In the midst of everything coming apart, I started studying the Bible rapaciously. When I look back at that first Study Bible and see the things I found important (I am a big Bible highlighter), I realize that the person who read that Bible doesn't exist today. The connections made by the study notes in that decidedly evangelical Study Bible made perfect sense to me back then, but there are very few of those connections I can still endorse. The important thing was that my love for the scriptures was kindled. I soon came across books that taught me historical critical biblical scholarship and left my evangelical perspective behind, the Bible in the process only becoming richer for me. I soon moved back to Milwaukee and returned to school, with dual majors in Biblical Theology and Psychology. After graduation, I enrolled in graduate school in Religious Studies.

During the time I was finishing my undergraduate degree and doing graduate work, I worked in inpatient mental health. Actually, I started working in mental health in Indianapolis after leaving Field Service. There I managed a group home for Cognitively Impaired Adults. It was hospital work I did after returning to Milwaukee that I really loved, and it was also the best preparation for ministry I could ever have had. I worked at a suburban hospital that primarily served people who weren't extremely sick, though some were, and I also worked through an agency at other facilities, my favorite being St. Luke's in Racine, WI, which was the county hospital for Racine and Kenosha counties in southeastern Wisconsin. There I saw many people who were very sick, and I often reflected that there, but for a little bit of brain chemistry, would be each and every one of us.

Of course, to work in that kind of environment

you have to have a dark sense of humor or you won't survive. There are also things that happen that are objectively hilarious. One of my favorite stories involved a psychiatrist who was also a pastor. I'll call him Dr. Washburn. I loved Dr. Washburn, because although he was quite successful he still worked with the poor who had Medicaid for insurance, which paid almost nothing for care. I will never forget one patient in particular who was schizophrenic but had gotten pregnant and so stopped her medications because they would harm the baby. The sad truth was that an amniocentesis revealed that the baby had been harmed by the meds and was not likely to survive.

When this happened we didn't know that, and Dr. Washburn had put the patient in the hospital to keep her safe while off her meds. She was about five months pregnant. One night she was feeling agitated and so asked if she could sit in the quiet room. She laid down quietly on the bed and we left the door open, checking on her every five minutes. On one check we discovered she had taken off all of her clothes. If you have ever seen the movie The Dream Team, you know this is not a good sign. She then started punching the wall above her head as she lay on the bed, bloodying her knuckles in the process. I was working with a guy named Scott, who was a body builder, that night and we both were in the room trying to calm her down. She started jumping up and down and thrashing about. Because she was pregnant, we wanted to be gentle, so Scott and I each grabbed one of her arms. This woman was not small, and we were being so gentle pretty soon we were nearly flying through the air, holding onto her arms for dear life. The nurse came in the room and told us to put her on her back on the bed due to her pregnancy. This is where it got really ugly.

We put her on her back on the bed. The thing to do with a combative patient is to lay across their major muscle groups so they become fatigued and can't fight as much. One person lays across the patient's chest – or in this case because it was a naked pregnant woman, holds her shoulders. The other lays across her thighs. I should mention that schizophrenic patients often don't have the best hygiene. Fortunately, I got the shoulders. Dr. Washburn, who was in the hospital and had been called, ran into the room and the patient shouted, "Dr. Washburn, drop your pants and show me you're a man!" My shoulders were shaking almost as much as they did in that Methodist Church. She then began singing in a beautiful alto voice, alternating between a line of The Lord's Prayer and a profound sexual obscenity.

The next day a young female family doctor came in to do a pelvic examination on the patient. She found a hearing aid, a battery, and a watch in the patient's vagina. I asked the unsuspecting doctor whether the watch was still working. She said she didn't check, and asked why I wanted to know. I told her I was just wondering if it was a Timex. Dark humor relieves a lot of stress.

At the time I was working in hospitals and finishing my undergraduate degree, I really believed I was called to be an Episcopal Priest. Had the process gone well for me I believe I would have been a fine Episcopal Priest. As it turned out, the process revealed to me so much of what was wrong with the system – not just in the Episcopal Church, but in every denomination or non-denomination that uses such a system – that I was left with a choice of living in the same kind of dysfunction I grew up with or moving on. I now see that, in a counterintuitive way, becoming an Episcopal Priest might well have destroyed me.

As I moved through the discernment process, I came to understand that for me that process had very little to do with God and everything to do with politics and antiquated understandings of human nature and psychology. I have to say, having resigned from the process nearly fifteen years ago now, that it was so profoundly unhealthy psychologically – and I have found many others since that time that have been through various mainline Protestant discernment processes who agree – that it borders on being evil. Aspirants for Ordination are required to share their life story with complete strangers who are untrained in hearing such stories. Personal boundaries are not only disrespected, they must be discarded if one is to engage the process with any hope of success. Conflicts of interest among people involved in the process are ignored rather than resulting in those with a conflict of interest excusing themselves from the proceedings, and cronyism abounds. Fortunately for me, I had the educational and vocational background to recognize how unhealthy the process was and chose to withdraw after the bishop told me "people like you can never be normal." He was referring to my abuse history, and his perspective was the product of misinformation and folklore that remained unchanged even as I cited the research data that disproved his superstition. He offered me the option of seeing one of several psychologist friends of his who were not covered by my insurance for a year and then to come back to see him. Since I had released all of my medical records to his office, including my therapy records, I didn't see much point in seeing his friend who apparently needed the work. What's more, I couldn't afford to pay out of pocket for a year of therapy that I had already done, and had ethical issues with buying my way to ordination by paying a psychologist several thousand dollars out-of-pocket, even if I could have afforded it. As they say in the recovery movement, insanity is doing the same thing over and over and expecting different results. I often think about the many people who don't see the damage they are inflicting on themselves by participating in the process, and pray that they may recover their lost dignity before inflicting similar damage on those whom they serve in ministry.

Not long after withdrawing from the process in the Episcopal Church and while doing graduate work at Cardinal Stritch University, I received a call to serve a worshiping community that had broken from the Roman Catholic Church in the late 1960s. There were at one time hundreds if not thousands of these churches across the country that had left Rome when their local parish refused to implement the changes called for in Vatican II. These people, for reasons that may be hard to us to imagine today, loved the folk Mass. Easier to comprehend is their love for social justice. In December of 1999 I was ordained, finally serving as priest in a place I never knew existed back when my journey to ordination began in that United Methodist pastor's office some sixteen years earlier. At the same time, I knew that this single, insular, somewhat inbred congregation that hadn't seen a new member in more than a decade was dying a slow death of attrition. In fact, they had told me as much during the interview process. I started looking for an organization that I could become a part of that would afford me the opportunity to serve beyond the life of my part time call to this aging congregation. As it turned out, the organizations that existed at the time didn't fit my evolving spirituality.

I had become radically inclusive. Through a series of life events, I had come to learn and experience that, when the chips were down, it was my gay and lesbian friends who had my back. As I had gotten more in touch with my history of sexual abuse, my heterosexual friends abandoned me. In the recovery group that I found, I learned that my gay and lesbian friends in that group *could* hear my story without running away. The same was true later in life when I worked in inpatient mental health. When things got physical, it was mostly my LGBT coworkers who were with me in the middle of the action, while most of my heterosexual coworkers cowered in the corner. I resolved never to abandon any of God's children, most especially those who had been there for me in my times of need.

In the late 1980s, I had read Bishop John Shelby Spong's critically important book <u>Living in Sin?</u>, and had at long last found a voice within the Church that agreed with how I felt about not only human sexuality, but divorce, cohabitation, and the need to develop rituals that honor all of life's transitions. As a member of the Episcopal Church in the mid 1990s, I was extremely vocal in my opposition to the Walter Righter heresy trial, which sought to defrock then retired Bishop Righter and take away his pension and health care because he had ordained an openly gay man a deacon. I couldn't believe the hate that would cause an allegedly Christian organization to attempt to leave a retired clergyman with a lifetime of service to the Church without retirement or medical care because of one act. While there certainly were inclusive churches that existed at the time, most of them were inclusive of the LGBT community but exclusive of heterosexuals! That left me out!

I had also become interspiritual. That first church I took in 1999 that I described earlier had a tradition of an annual Lenten book study. As any good pastor seeking to understand a new community might do, I asked what they had read the year before my arrival. The answer was <u>Living Buddha, Living Christ</u> by Thich Nhat Hahn. I had no idea who Thich Nhat Hahn was and knew next to nothing of Buddhism. I ordered the book and read it, and my life was transformed. I became a student of Buddhism, which made sense of the contemplative life in a way that Christian teachings had been unable to for me. For those who don't know, Buddhism offers a way of working with our minds that can be taken as a religious practice, but doesn't have to be. It can be a valuable part of our spiritual practice no matter our background, especially since Buddhism is silent on the concept of God. Admittedly, it would be hard to study Buddhism while holding to a conservative Christian belief in an interventionist God. Since that wasn't my perspective, I had no problem adapting.

In the summer of 2003 I came across a discussion on the website of what was then called The Universal Anglican Church of America. There were, in the beginning, five co-founders. I was elected Presiding Bishop in February of 2004, and formally seated by Bishop Joseph Rose at our first General Assembly in October of 2004. We were founded as a radically inclusive, mixed Church – by which we meant that it was our goal to include representatives of all segments of society. In our estimation, when the Church closes her doors on anyone, she is in error. You don't solve the problem of bigotry and exclusion by setting up an organization that is bigoted and exclusive in the other direction. In fact, such policies only make the situation worse by supporting the very small mindedness they claim to abhor. We were resolved to not make that mistake in the Universal Anglican Church. We also had resolved to focus our attention on issues of social justice. We came to that decision through a close reading of the Gospels and the prophets. We were convinced that God has a devotion, even a preferential option, for the poor and marginalized and that Jesus did, too. We resolved to share that devotion.

In the beginning, we believed that we were forming a denomination with Anglican Spirituality – and indeed, we did precisely that. Over time we began to consider the truth that if we were going to exclude someone because they didn't believe exactly the way we did, we no longer qualified as an inclusive organization. Historic Anglicanism has always been light on doctrine, believing that great benefit and learning comes from the creative tension that exists when people of differing beliefs live and worship together. We began pushing that envelope. As more people joined the conversation, we became more and more diverse – and more and more pluralistic. We also began living into the fullness of our name.

Originally, we called ourselves the Universal Anglican Church in America. The "in America" was dropped within a few months as we realized that it was a contradiction to claim to be Universal and then limit ourselves to America. We used the word "Universal" because we wanted to reflect the fact that we were allied with the small "c" catholic tradition. The meaning of the word catholic is "universal," and so our name included that word. As we grew and evolved, more and more of us discovered, after studying the scriptures and a long period of reflection and prayer, that we were universalists – meaning that all people are loved by God and that there is no such thing as hell. We had come to see the truth that Jesus never used the word "hell" in the original language of the New Testament. Rather, he used the word Gehenna, which referred to the garbage dump outside the city walls of Jerusalem. In fact, the notion of hell is foreign to the Jewish tradition in which Jesus lived, moved, and had his being. People who died were thought to go to Sheol, which was a place a lot like a state of limbo rather than an eternal torture chamber. Our vision, and our inclusivity, had broadened.

At this point in time, although unbeknownst to me, there was still more growth in my future. Hopefully, there always will be! In October of 2009 during the General Assembly of The Universal Anglican Church, we took a field trip of sorts to Hubertis, Wisconsin and Holy Hill, which is the National Shrine of Mary, Help of Christians. It is also the highest point in southeastern Wisconsin, and a wonderful place from which to observe the fall colors. It is, as its name implies, a very holy place. While praying in one of the side chapels off of the main church, I heard a voice calling me to "build it." I had no idea what it was that I was supposed to build, and I didn't feel the least bit like Kevin Kostner in "Field of Dreams," but I was convinced that the message was genuine. Over the next several weeks, it became clear to me that so much of institutional Christianity spent nearly all of its time talking about Salvation – despite the fact that Jesus never talked about Salvation in the same sense that the institution does, of being saved from hell. What Jesus *did* talk about could be more accurately described as wisdom and enlightenment teachings that urged people to create the Kingdom of God on earth. No hellfire, no damnation, just the creation of heaven on earth.

The truth is that institutional Christianity is in trouble. Research shows that, despite the claims of the faithful when interviewed, people aren't going to church any more. Half of Roman Catholics claim they attend church on a weekly basis, but parish attendance figures show that only twenty-eight percent of them are actually present. Protestant attendance is worse, with forty percent claiming they are in church weekly, while in reality only half that number are actually in attendance. We could look at the truth that half of the people who say they are in church are lying as some evidence of failure to teach the Ten Commandments, but it's much more likely that the disparity reflects a fair amount of guilt on the part of those not present. People seem to feel that they *should* be present, or that the interviewer or others will think poorly of them if they aren't in church, and so claim they are present. Roughly averaging the above percentages and factoring in the fact that ninety-six percent of Americans say they believe in God and eighty percent of Americans identify as Christians, the conclusion is that four out of five Americans are not going to church on a regular basis. The decline has been consistent over the last five decades.

These statistics raise a number of questions, many of which would be delightful fodder for a book, and many such books have been written. So-called "church growth experts" have written countless articles, manuals, and books filled with strategies and advice for pastors who want to see their churches grow. With the primary tool of evaluation for most pastors being church attendance and growth, we can be sure most of them are very concerned about church growth. Given the trend in the statistics, even when one church in town has an attendance increase, the overall number of people in church has continued to decline. That means that, even when churches do grow, they are growing at the expense of other churches in town and not because they have succeeded in drawing people in from the largest mission field available: The Church Alumni Association. This would seem to validate the somewhat cynical notion that church consultants exist not to solve problems but rather to make money while prolonging the difficulty.

If we look only at Christians, something I tend *not* to do because my understanding of God and spirituality transcends the human constructs of denominations and religions, three out of four Christians do not go to church regularly. Among conservative Christians the attendance numbers are slightly higher while among moderate and progressive

Christians the attendance numbers are slightly lower, but all are trending downward. With all of the efforts of all of the experts directed at getting at least some of the seventy-five percent of Christendom back in the door, why aren't they succeeding?

The answer isn't simple, nor is there a quick fix. If there was, it would have been discovered and implemented long ago. It's not as if changing one thing about church would change everything. It's not even the case that there exists a universal answer, that if we just did these three or four things then half of those currently not in church would return. It's not even as if the problem is universal. In the global South the church is growing, while in Western Europe the decline in church attendance and involvement occurred much earlier than it has in North America. European Cathedrals, some of the most beautiful examples of humanity being inspired by their experience of God and responding by building enormous worship centers that seem to reach to the very heavens, have been empty for years.

Some years ago, while shopping for a greeting

card in a little artsy card shop in Newburyport, Massachusetts, I came across a card which has stayed with me. On the front of the card was a hard boiled egg, sitting in a cardboard stand and decorated to look like a farmer. The egg was wearing a flannel shirt and denim overalls, had a straw hat on its head and a hayseed sticking out of its mouth. I opened the card and read, "It's hard to keep them on the farm once they have been laid."

Elvis has left the building, and untold effort has been wasted trying to get the genie back into the bottle. As for me, I love church. I love to worship and love everything about worship. I love the beautiful music of the church both traditional and contemporary, but I have discovered something the church in all its forms needs to hear: People aren't buying what you are selling anymore. The truth is that the institutional church is much like the Titanic. It imagines itself impervious to destruction, it doesn't exactly turn on a dime, and entrenched within its hallowed halls are people who have a vested interest in maintaining the status quo. It has shifted its attention from the Global North to the

Global South, foolishly believing that the Global South won't come to the very place where the European Church did several decades ago and where the North American Church has arrived within the last few decades. There is no evidence of the Church responding to the needs of the people on any significant scale, and there is no reason to believe that situation is going to change, save in certain small corners of the church universal that have avoided becoming institutions.

Over the past thirty years I have come to learn that the God of my experience is not the God of the institutional Church. The fact that in the middle of the last decade of the twentieth century I was told by a mainline Protestant bishop that I could never be normal because I had been abused as a child reflects a profound lack of faith in both God and the human condition. Either redemption *is* possible or it isn't, and the belief that it *is* possible is a central tenant of the Christian faith. The bishop's view of God and humanity was completely inconsistent with the God I had come to know and love, as well as the message of Christianity that there is redemption and healing in Jesus Christ! A

Church that has a bishop who doesn't believe in change is a Church in trouble, indeed!

As a priest and bishop of a decidedly non-institutional Church, I have come to learn that what I suspected was true. It is not only possible, but also critically important, to engage people in a discussion about the God of their experience. I have discovered that I am far from alone in my understanding of the proper role of spirituality, as opposed to religion, in the lives of people. The most gratifying moments of my ministry have been the countless opportunities I have had to affirm people in their experience of God. These moments are also the most heart rending, because before being able to affirm their experience of God I must hear their stories of being wounded by the Church. I must tell them what they already suspect, but no clergy person in their experience has had the courage and integrity to say – that the things the Church did that wounded them should never have happened. They should not have been rejected by their church because they couldn't afford nice clothes to wear on Sunday morning, or because their parents were divorced, or because they lived in the wrong part of town. Their mother should not have been denied Communion because she left their father who was an alcoholic and had beaten her and her children repeatedly. Their pastor should not have come to their home while they were at work and spoken to their boyfriend or girlfriend, trying to convince them to move out of the home they shared because they were "living in sin." Their child should not have been refused baptism because his or her parents weren't married. The list of offenses seems to be endless, and when I tell people these things should never have happened and apologize to them on behalf of the Church, many of them weep.

The problem is not that the Church isn't offering the right music, quality sermons, convenient worship times, good child care during worship, or dry cleaning in the lobby. It may or may not be doing those things, but the real problem is that the understanding of God offered by the Church no longer resonates with the people the church attempts to reach. In my travels I have found many who have left church in search of God, and who in fact were only able to find God after leaving church. Many are still looking, and it is my sincere hope that this book might, in some small way, contribute to the search for God which I believe is a part of every human being, whether or not they call the objective of their search "God."

6 SPIRITUAL BUT NOT RELIGIOUS?

We hear quite a few contemporary people saying that they are "spiritual but not religious," (SBNR) and they are in fact the fastest growing segment of the American spiritual landscape, but there are probably as many different meanings for that label as there are people who claim it. Many of the meanings are obvious, such as when we hear someone use that expression right after someone has invited them to attend their church. "Thank you anyway, but I'm spiritual, not religious," means, "leave me alone, you obnoxious boor". Others use the expression almost apologetically as if they had to explain why they don't go to church. Still others say spiritual but not religious in an attempt to define their spirituality. The problem with all of this is that it doesn't really say very much about one's spiritual life at all because it primarily says what a person *isn't*. After it's said, neither party to the conversation has a much better idea about the beliefs or spiritual journey of the other.

What are SBNR people saying? A few years ago I was in Hartford, Connecticut for the annual meeting of my brother from another mother, Bishop John L. Selders, Jr. We had some free time after the conference had ended so John, his wife Pamela, my wife Erin, and I took a drive in the countryside. We came across a metaphysical shop and stopped in. The owner was a delightful woman who, upon learning we were clergy, told us that she very much loved and believed in Jesus, but had to leave the Church to find him. Her statement stayed with me for some reason, and I thought about it often over the next few weeks. I didn't disagree with her at all, and I started to reflect on why it was the case that some people had to leave the Church to find God. I had done a presentation at the annual General Assembly of The Universal Anglican Church that demonstrated that we were creating a convergence in our work between our liturgical heritage, the social justice movement, and the openness to the Spirit that is characteristic of charismatic churches. Now, upon doing some research, I learned that eighty percent of America was not in church on a regular basis, a fact that aligned with what the woman at the metaphysical shop had shared of her own experience. I sat with this and came to some conclusions about the difference between religion and spirituality, beginning with the truth that there is overlapping ground between religion and spirituality.

Churches tend to have a formal membership process; a set of beliefs (whether few or many) in which one must profess belief to become a member and/or stay a member; a system of pledging and/or contributing in which one is expected to participate when one becomes a member; and from which one can be expelled should one violate the expectations of the parish or denomination. Members and visitors may or may not be encouraged or allowed to ask questions of the authority figure, who is most often a member of the ordained clergy. Depending on the tradition, clergy may be appointed by the denomination, called by the members of the parish, or called by the parish with denominational approval. Most often there is a formal hierarchy within these parishes, with ordained clergy at the top followed by some sort of board elected by the membership. How a member is expected to relate to the ordained clergy and lay leadership of the parish varies from organization to organization, but generally speaking there is some amount of deference to the clergy by the membership. There are also varying levels of questioning of and diversity in belief that is tolerated. The central events of parish life are worship opportunities, and there is an expectation that members will perform acts of service within the institution as well as in the community with the former often being stressed to the exclusion of the latter. Loyalty to the congregation and/or denomination is stressed (though denominational loyalty has declined dramatically over the last few decades), and to a certain extent the primary goal of the organization is to perpetuate itself. Do something to threaten the life of the organization in the eyes of its power brokers, and out you go. As you might imagine, these structures of institutional religion tend to work against freedom of thought and belief, sometimes even against honest inquiry.

As I mentioned, spirituality is often but not always a part of institutional religion. When people talk about being spiritual but not religious, it's often because they have been wounded to one extent or another by the hierarchy, doctrine, or dogma of religion. Many of us know people who are very angry with the Roman Catholic Church because when they were children their parents divorced and their mother was unable to receive the Sacraments because she remarried. So, when people talk about being SBNR, they are saying they practice their spirituality in a way that most likely is less formally structured than religion. People who identify as spiritual do very often gather in community, but the structure of the communities in which they gather is much more diverse and the gatherings may or may not be designated as expressly spiritual. There still may be a fair amount of teaching or instruction, but generally speaking spirituality allows the individual receiving the teaching to receive it in a way that allows her to take what she needs and leave the rest. There tend to be fewer, if any, required beliefs although there are generally shared beliefs that bind the community together. The teacher, who may still be a member of the ordained clergy or equivalent, is seen in a less hierarchical manner. Instead, the teacher is seen as journeying with and sharing information rather than dispensing truth from on high. Questions are not only allowed but encouraged. There most likely is a meeting place, but it does not necessarily belong to the congregation and may instead be shared, rented or leased. Membership may be much less formal, and the definition of membership may be that one considers oneself a member. While donations are encouraged to support the work of the teacher or clergy, formal pledge drives as such often are not a part of spiritual communities. The clergy may be bi-vocational, receiving a small stipend from the community and earning the majority of their income from another job. None of this is to say that spiritual communities don't have systems of organization or styles of relating one to another, but it is to say that these things tend to develop more organically from within the organization rather then being structure being imposed from outside. Acts of service may tend to be emphasized and encouraged outside the context of the community rather than within. There is nothing about visiting another spiritual center that would be seen as disloyal.

The truth is that in most churches and spiritual centers a small percentage of the members, somewhere between five and ten percent of members, do the vast majority of the work. The same people volunteer for committees over and over, and so effectively hold most of the power. I have always been of the opinion that our love of committees has done more to stand in the way of progress than any other single entity in spiritual life. I am reminded of a story about church committees and practices.

It seems there was a small town, and on the corners of the intersection of the main streets there were three churches – one Methodist, one Evangelical, and one Episcopal - and the town hall. The town hall had a problem with bats in their bell tower. They had called every exterminator in town but couldn't get rid of the bats. Finally, desperate to rid themselves of the problem, they contacted the Evangelical Church and asked if they could help.

The Evangelical Church was glad to report they could indeed help. They marched across the street with their prayer warriors and cast the demons out of those bats, who promptly left the bell tower only to return one day later. The Evangelical Church reported with sadness there was nothing more that could be done, so the Town contacted the Methodists.

Indeed, the Methodists had the solution! They formed a committee to study the bats and bat habitats. They learned that bats lived in caves, and so they went to the outskirts of town and found a suitable cave. The women's guild made lovely curtains for the cave, crocheted nice warm blankets for the bats, and made some lovely crafts with which to decorate the cave. Then they went to the bell tower, captured the bats and released them in their lovely new home. One week later, the bats were back. In desperation, the Town contacted the Episcopal Church.

The Episcopalians gathered for cocktails – as Episcopalians are wont to do – then called in the choir, the acolytes, the vestry, and the priests. They all vested in their finest vestments, the thurifer fired up the incense, they took a large pot of Holy water, and singing "Lift High the Cross" they processed across the street to the Town Hall. Still singing, they climbed the bell tower. The priests then baptized the bats, and they haven't been seen or heard from since!

My life experience has certainly led me to consider myself more spiritual than religious. From those days in the Congregational Church to the day my bishop in the Episcopal Church told me I could never be normal, religion had not been a particularly welcoming place. On the other hand, I had developed a rich spirituality and had a deep love of God. You might say that I hadn't rejected the goal of the spiritual life, union with the Divine, but I had largely rejected the vehicle that had historically been assigned to carry people to the goal - even as I was the founding bishop of just such a vehicle! While we had initially seen ourselves as a relatively traditional denomination in terms of structure we were radically non-traditional in our radical openness and inclusivity. I suppose under the circumstances it would not have been possible for us to have retained an extremely traditional structure or our inclusivity would have been compromised. Fortunately, I had brought with me a dislike for five and ten year plans. When I was working in the medical field in my twenties, my supervisors always wanted to know were I hoped to be in five and ten years. My experience had been that my life was so volatile there was no point in making those plans, that it was far better to be open to whatever came along and adjust and adapt to life on its own terms. Later I would learn that my openness to change was actually a much healthier process than trying to control reality and resist change. In fact, it's part of what Buddhists mean when they talk about non-attachment.

The truth is that religion, like people in general, tends to resist change and when change does happen it moves very slowly and with great weeping, wailing, and gnashing of teeth in implementing the change. It doesn't matter how great or small the change, change usually means some members will leave a church. When I was an Episcopalian we used to love the joke about how man Episcopalians it takes to change a light bulb. The answer? "Change? My grandmother gave that bulb to the church!" On the other hand, my experience with SBNR folk is that they actually *want* to try new things because a great number of them have found the intransigence of religion very stifling. They *want* more freedom, not less, especially when it comes to exploring new ideas and beliefs. However, they are no less afraid of change than the population at large and so once a spiritual group has been formed it, too, may well try to codify beliefs and resist change. The only way to avoid such a problem is to ensure a constant flow of new ideas and faces into the community and recognize that new members bring with them new perspectives and beliefs which must be honored and respected. That can be easier said than done. I believe the key is to consistently talk about change being an unavoidable fact of life. Any group that becomes isolated and closed is on its way to a death by attrition. I once served an independent church that had originally been quite radical and innovative, but over the years had closed in on itself and become very isolated and inbred. While imagining themselves quite open and friendly, they drove away anyone who visited because they were unwilling to accept their ideas, unwilling to consider any kind of change to worship, and absolutely opposed to new people serving on their board even as they "complained" about having to do all the work themselves. When they did allow new people to serve, they insisted on conformity through the practice of expressing extreme displeasure rather passive-aggressively if people voted against the majority or introduced new ideas.

We face a contemporary spiritual climate, then, in which contemporary seekers are not willing to put their minds on hold in order to conform to the expectations of the institution. That being said, most of them have nevertheless been shaped by the institution. No longer are people willing to sit by and not ask the questions that they wrestle with or to pretend to believe in something they find unlikely just to fit in. However, when they leave they may be tempted to set up equally dysfunctional spirituality centers across town. Despite what might be called bad organizations habits that need to be replaced, the truth is that advances in scientific knowledge have led faithful people to struggle with accepting parts of the Christian mythos that are in conflict with that knowledge. When an institution insists that its members continue to hold beliefs while ignoring their doubts, believers respond by leaving. What's more, the widespread corruption of corporate culture in America and throughout the world coupled with the institution-wide corruption of the Roman Catholic Church has forever damaged the credibility of institutions of all types. While the mantra of the 1960s may have been, "Question Authority," a contemporary mantra may well be, "Question Institutional Authority." Both questions are important and essential on the spiritual journey!

How do we do spiritual community in this context? Do we throw out the baby with the bathwater? Do we just adopt practices and beliefs from other traditions and ignore the fact that the cultural religious experience of most westerners is Judeo-Christian? What has happened to Christianity, and what can we learn from it as we move forward into the SBNR future? What are the factors pushing against business as usual?

7 THE TIMES ARE CHANGING

Much of the institutional Christian world sees the changing spiritual landscape as a problem, but in truth it is nothing more than a stage in the development of the Christian spiritual path. Not liking change never stopped it. There are some major challenges that face the aspiring clergy person today, but if they are addressed properly they need not be a detriment to the spiritual life. In fact, those challenges may just open up the faith of our ancestors in ways they could not possibly have imagined. The days when the small town pastor could rest on her laurels, secure in the knowledge that her flock was Christian and always would be, that they would never even accidentally stumble across another tradition and so all she had to do was keep them loyal to their denomination are gone for good. The Dalai Lama is one of the most recognizable figures in the world, and that recognition has brought with it at least a passing awareness of Buddhism. For tens of thousands of Americans the awareness has been more than passing, as Buddhism together with Islam are the fastest growing religions in the United States. The reason is that both Buddhism and Islam offer a system of belief that impacts every corner of the practitioner's life and a practice that is available on a twenty-four hours a day, seven day a week basis. We need to ask ourselves how we can make Christianity a practice based spirituality that isn't just a Sunday morning event. What might a daily Christian spiritual practice be?

The events of September 11, 2001 have caused many people to want to understand Islam and the role that Islamic fundamentalism played in the actions of the terrorists who attacked the United States on that day. Battles about human sexuality and its implications for faith communities have been front and center even before the consecration of The Rt. Rev. V. Gene Robinson of New Hampshire as the first openly gay, non-celibate Bishop in the Episcopal Church. Mormonism has seen increased awareness since the Mormon Church became actively involved in the legal battle against marriage equality in California, and Warren Jeffs and the FLDS drew attention as well for alleged practices of forced marriage of minor children to significantly older men. Then there is Mitt Romney. This list isn't meant to be comprehensive, merely to show through a brief review of recent news how much the spiritual landscape is changing and how poorly pastors are prepared to handle the change.

This isn't a book for pastors, however. It is a book for people on a spiritual journey. Hopefully that list includes pastors, but it doesn't include all of them. If you are a person who is perfectly happy going to the church you have gone to for some years now; if the fact that there aren't nearly the same number of people at worship that there used to be is just fine with you; and if you are a member of the rare congregation that isn't struggling to make ends meet; this book may not be for you. On the other hand, if you have noticed that the three biggest line items in the parish budget are staff salaries, the apportionment you pay to the denomination, and building mortgage and maintenance, and as a result you cannot find a way to squeeze out any money to do ministry; or if you worry about what your spiritual life is going to look like when the day comes when you can't get to church on Sunday morning because Sunday morning is the only time that building you are paying so much for is used for spiritual purposes, then you might just want to keep reading!

I began to see that something was very wrong with the way we conduct business as church in America back in the late 1990s. I was a member of an Episcopal parish that had so much trouble passing a budget that they omitted ministry to the community from the budget. If they were going to do any outreach they would pay for it with bake sales, rummage sales, and other fundraisers throughout the year. The problem is that if you take outreach out of the parish budget your building suddenly changes from a church into a country club. Some would say that the situation I describe is unusual, but they would be mistaken. In fact, most American churches are run on the country club model, and their members are just fine with that way of being church (which isn't really being church at all). The problem is that Country Clubs have very restrictive membership policies, and the Church is supposed to be welcoming, isn't it?

Some years ago I heard a story about an Episcopal

priest who was hired to be the rector of a parish in Texas that had decided they wanted to grow. This poor fellow took that church at their word, and in his first year as rector he added two hundred fifty members to the parish – and got fired for that accomplishment. He got fired because he brought in the *wrong people*. What was wrong with them? The parish thought they were problematic because they weren't from the same socio-economic class as the existing membership, some of them were unemployed, others were in recovery from addiction, and some were homeless. This story is all about church as country club, which seems pretty strange given that a cursory reading of the Gospel makes it pretty clear that the people that parish rejected are precisely the people in whose company Jesus spent the vast majority of his time on earth.

Another church fancied itself very welcoming and accommodating. Having in the last decade conducted a major addition to the parish which included a new fellowship hall with a full sized commercial kitchen, this parish held their adult education sessions between worship services in that fellowship hall. Each Sunday members ate pastries and washed them down with coffee, tea, and juice while listening to erudite presentations from members of the parish, clergy, local seminary faculty, or other local personalities of note. About halfway through the presentation each week a local homeless man entered the fellowship hall and was completely ignored as he made his way around the back of the assembly to the refreshment table. He helped himself to a couple of pastries and a cup of coffee and left the way he had entered. The parish prided itself on being very welcoming and generous in allowing this man to partake of their refreshments. Despite their self-perceived generosity, nobody ever greeted the man and he was never invited to have a seat and stay a while. He didn't fit in with the self perception of the parish as country club. Interestingly, this same parish had a member who was police lieutenant who served as an usher. If someone entered the narthex (lobby) that didn't fit the image of a member of this church, the policeman would flash his badge and frisk the person in question.

My intent in relaying these stories is not to be

overly harsh or judgmental. It is certainly true that human beings prefer to gather and worship with people with whom they share some commonalities, and there isn't anything wrong with that tendency per se. What is interesting about the anecdotes related above is how inconsistent they are with the self image of the parishes in question. That points out that, in general, we are not very good at self-evaluation. It also points out that gradually we have drifted from who we once were as faith communities. The local church that was once the center of community life now sits empty six and one half days a week. The exception to this rule is the fortunate church that has succeeded in leasing part of its building to a day care center. Research shows that more than seventy percent of American Protestant churches worship less that one hundred twenty five people on Sunday. One hundred people are barely enough to pay a full time pastor. Churches are reaching into their endowment funds to stay afloat, mortgaging a future that will never come. The vast majority of Christians think of their faith as something they plug into on Sunday morning and ignore the rest of the week. That isn't indicative of a problem with Christians, rather it belies a problem with the Church. Institutional Christianity is surviving only because it is on life support thanks to endowments, and it is long past time to pull the plug.

As I alluded to earlier, I grew up in a large Congregational church – an independent Congregational church, not one that was a part of the United Church of Christ. I have already told the story, but now I would like to examine what happened there from an organizational perspective. Sunday school classes taught the same lessons over and over, year after year, using the same methods that the academic classroom used except that the teachers were not trained as teachers and the technology was outdated. We were being taught the story of the Hebrew and early Christian people without any attempt to connect it to our lives. Spirituality wasn't part of the experience at all. It's very little wonder that I found church boring and irrelevant – it was! The sad truth is that while the technology has improved and new programs of learning have been created that have the ability to hold children's attention a bit longer, Sunday schools still aren't teaching spirituality. Why not? I believe it's because we aren't teaching spirituality in the Sanctuary or in adult education, either. We are teaching salvation, which has already happened, as if it was a goal that we have to work toward. When clergy are asked about prayer the most common response is a look of terror that they are being asked to explain something that is completely beyond their experience.

In liturgical churches the clergy often talk about the importance of a life of prayer for clergy. They tend to see that prayer as praying the daily office or the liturgy of the hours, perhaps praying the rosary or something similar, and offering intercessory prayer for their parishioners, friends, and family. While all of this is certainly prayer, it might be described as a prayer primer. Like memorized prayers that we say when asked to offer a blessing over food, they require very little depth of feeling or thought. When one has prayed the liturgy of the hours for thirty days or so – about the time it takes to figure out how to use the ribbon markers that make using the book efficiently possible – one has learned about all they need to know to pull off praying the hours in a group without embarrassing themselves. Most people who feel they may be called upon to offer grace over a meal pretty quickly develop a standard prayer for the purpose. None of this, in and of itself, constitutes a life of prayer, although in fairness we might say that all of the aforementioned practices may very well be *part* of a life of prayer. The shocking thing is that for most if not all of institutional Christianity no attempt is made to explore prayer beyond this introductory level, and no attempt is made to require clergy to develop a deep life of prayer! That leaves the average clergy person profoundly unqualified to teach prayer to those they encounter who yearn for it. This despite the fact that very often in the Gospels Jesus went away to a quiet place and spent the night in prayer. He was not carrying a copy of a daily office prayer book with him!

Feeling the church is irrelevant or an alienating presence in life is a problem for many people regardless of their background, age, or socioeconomic circumstance. The problem exists when couples divorce and one gets custody of the church. Usually, but not always, the woman gets custody. I have never believed it is the job of the church to take sides in situations like these, rather I believe the job of the church is to do all she can to ensure that all parties involved emerge whole. I once knew a man who was profoundly physically abused by his wife. He spent a summer trying to set things right in their relationship, and he spent that summer with a torso and upper arms covered in bruises. The last straw for him came when she tried to penetrate him rectally with a broom stick while he slept. He left the next day, fearing for his life and having to move several towns away to feel safe. While it would have been dangerous for him to return to his home church and so you might say he voluntarily surrendered it, he came to me to discuss his sadness after his former pastor called to chastise him for leaving his marriage.

The problem for divorcing couples is intensified by churches that refuse one or both partners the sacraments because they are divorced or who are actually thrown out of their church home for being divorced. Couples who are living together and seeking to live the spiritual life are also often victimized by people, ordained and laity, who seek to impose the will of the system on their lives. The same is true for lesbian, gay, bisexual, and transgender people who are very often the victims of hate speech by ignorant fellow parishioners who speak out at meetings about how violent they would be toward any one of *those people* should they ever show up. I watched just such a display by a member of an Episcopal Church in the mid 1990s, when the chancellor made such an announcement completely oblivious that he was sitting next to a partnered lesbian with whom he sat on the vestry.

I'm not for a moment suggesting that any of the people I have described were ill intended, or incompetent, unintelligent, or anything else negative. They all believed they were acting as their faith compelled them to act. They were doing the best they could within the system in which they were working. The problem existed not with the good people of the parishes I have described, nor with the people of any congregation of any denomination. The problem was and is within the system itself. The only question that remains is whether or not the system can be repaired, or if it will require so much effort to repair that we would be better served to start over..

8 HOW THINGS WERE

If you were raised as a Christian, I invite you to pause a moment and reflect on whether you were taught your faith tradition as a set of facts or stories to be memorized or a practice to be learned. In your experience as a Christian, was how you felt more important or was what you knew more important? If you come from an evangelical background, the chances are that memorizing Bible passages was emphasized, as was debating people who were not practicing Christians. In truth, "practicing Christians" were most likely defined as Christians who went to the same kind of church that you attended. Did the teaching you received, whether through the sermons that were preached or the classes that were taught, focus more on the Old Testament, the New Testament, or was there an equal balance between the two? What was the view of other Christians? If you were Protestant what was the view of Catholics, and if you were Catholic what was the view of Protestants? What was the view of non-

Christians? Other than attending worship services and education classes at your place of worship, what other practices were taught as being an essential part of your faith?

These questions help us start to identify the religious environment in which we were raised or in which we worship as adults. Even if you have no exposure to the Christian tradition, these questions serve to provide something of an overview of the diversity that exists within institutional Christianity even as they barely scratch the surface. Perhaps the pivotal question among many Christians has been around the proper relationship between faith and works. Are we saved by faith alone, as Martin Luther suggested (and edited his translation of the Bible to say) or do our actions have an impact? One of the questions I am trying to answer is, "How do we address the faith vs. works question when we come to realize we are all saved already?" In fact, how is the spiritual journey changed when we accept the fact that Jesus was primarily a wisdom and enlightenment teacher whose primary message was that there is nothing we could ever do to separate us from the Love that is God?

By now your head is probably spinning. You may well be thinking that this directly contradicts most if not all of what you were taught in your institutional Church, and you are correct! You may be thinking that this is some new age teaching, a corruption of the message of Jesus. In that you would be incorrect. This message is in fact very old. It extends to the first two to three centuries of Christianity, before Christianity was legalized and made the official religion of the Empire by Emperor Constantine. This view was held by very important figures in the early Church, St. Gregory of Nyssa and Origen among them. There was great diversity in the early years of Christianity, but that diversity disappeared when Christianity was institutionalized by the government in the early fourth century. Once anything becomes institutionalized and systematized diversity becomes problematic and assent to authority becomes valued above all else. The very strategy that worked so well in spreading Christianity also killed (sometimes quite literally) dissent and free thought. The institutional Church, not the Holy Spirit, spoke on God's behalf. Since the vast majority of the Christian faithful were illiterate and books were prohibitively expensive because they had to be hand copied, most people were happy to have the church tell them what to believe and how to behave. The problems with such a model are legion, but it took many years and a few fairly radical changes in the way people live for the problems to show themselves for what they are – life denying and suffocating, and when taken to an extreme, evil.

It's not within the purpose or scope of this book to chronicle the early years of the Church. For our purposes here it is important to note that quite a few of history's most regrettable moments were initiated by the Church in her misguided belief that the world needed to be conquered for God and the adherents of religions other than Christianity needed to be converted or killed. In fact, if one wonders how Islamic fundamentalists could possibly have attacked the (nominally) Christian United States, one need look no further than the Crusades fought by Christians attempting to reclaim the Holy Land from Islamic peoples by any means necessary, including genocide. Throughout the first fifteen hundred years of institutional Christianity the faithful seemed to just sit by passively and allow these things to happen. To believe that, however, would be to view the events of that time through the lens of twenty-first century technology and media. The common person didn't know what the Church was doing unless the Church wanted them to know. In the event of a major problem prior to the event of the printing press in 1440 C.E., there was no efficient way for the news to spread.

There was good news in the Church during this time as well as bad. The churches, particularly the monasteries, were the centers of education as well as spirituality and produced the brilliant minds of their day. Equally important was the ongoing practice of the life of prayer by monastics, a life of prayer that extended back to pre-Christian Judaism. Contemplative prayer, the Christian equivalent of what Eastern spirituality calls meditation, was carried on almost exclusively in the monasteries. It was believed that the common person could not practice contemplative prayer, and so no attempt was made to teach that very rich life of prayer to anyone living outside a monastic enclosure or hermitage. There were attempts to adapt something of monastic prayer life to the life of the faithful, however. The principal example of this was the rosary, which offered a way for the laity to offer one hundred fifty Hail Marys each day in parallel with the recitation of the entire Psalter of one hundred fifty Psalms in the monastery. Since the laity were illiterate it would have been almost impossible for them to recite the Psalter, but the rosary required only the use of prayers they had already memorized. The religious authorities of the day probably didn't expect that the rosary would turn into a doorway into contemplative prayer!

Every time I mention the Hail Mary I am reminded of the story of the Catholic parish that had both an all girls' and an all boys' High School attached. The day came when it was time for the boys to go to confession. As they huddled in the pews waiting for their turn and trying to come up with "sins" for which they wouldn't receive much in the way of penance,

Johnny was assuring his peers he had it all figured out. When his turn came, he marched into the confessional with a swagger that reflected his confidence.

He told the priest that he had been fooling around with a girl but that he was still something of a gentleman and wouldn't betray her identity to the priest. Johnny didn't kiss and tell. The priest asked, "Was it Mary?"

Johnny replied that it wasn't Mary, but that even if it had been he wouldn't tell the priest because he didn't kiss and tell. The priest asked if it had been Veronica and got the same reply from Johnny. Then he asked about Ruth. Johnny was mute. Finally the priest, a bit frustrated, told Johnny that while it would be better for his soul to tell him the name of the girl, he could still appreciate Johnny's integrity in refusing to name her. He told Johnny that he was banned from extra-curricular activities for three weeks and was to say ten Our Fathers and ten Hail Marys.

Upon exiting the confessional Johnny returned to his friends and they asked, "How'd you do?"

"Not too bad at all," replied Johnny, "I got three weeks off and three pretty good leads!"

Anyway, it was the aforementioned printing press that helped Martin Luther launch the Protestant Reformation in the early sixteenth century. Among the Reformers things Catholic were, and in some circles still are, regarded with suspicion at best and with hatred at worst. Ironically, the Protestant Reformation and the early stages of the Enlightenment that began one hundred years after the Reformation served as the one-two punch that nearly knocked the lights out of Christian mysticism. With the advent of the scientific method if something couldn't be observed and measured it didn't exist. This left all things spiritual suspect at best.

We need to pause a moment and examine the Reformation for what it was. To dismiss it as simply the result of the ill fated practice of selling indulgences or the desire of Henry VIII to divorce his wife is to completely misunderstand the Reformation. The broader motivation behind the Reformers was rather in reaction to the Catholic Church having significant land holdings and temporal power. It is important to remember that, with the exception of Orthodoxy in the east, the Catholic Church was the only Church prior to the Protestant Reformation. So intertwined with political power was the Church that Kings, not the Pope, often appointed bishops. At the other extreme, in places like England Henry VIII became very concerned that the Church owned more land in Henry's own country than Henry did! The Protestant Reformation, then, has to be seen not only as a reform of religious life but also as a reform of political life. Its immediate cause was abuse of power by the Church, but that was hardly the whole story. One of the sad results of the process was that when the bathwater that was the Church was thrown out, much of the baby of mystical spirituality went with it. Had not the monasteries survived, mystical spirituality might have been lost to Christianity forever. Even with the survival of the monasteries, mystical spirituality went underground and is only now beginning to emerge – no thanks to most of Christianity.

Another misconception about the Protestant Reformation is that it was an event much like flipping a light switch. Nothing could be farther from the truth. None of the four great Christian transformations to date were simple proclamations that were made one day and obeyed the next. The first great transformation was the reform of the early Church by Pope Gregory the Great, who is recognized as a saint in both the Roman and Orthodox Churches. He was the first Pope to come from the monastery, a prolific writer, and a Doctor of the Church, serving as Pope from 593 CE until his death in 610 CE. He faced a time of great conflict in the Church including threats of invasion that made it necessary for him to visit Constantinople and ask for the help of the Emperor in defending Rome. He also addressed the problem of clerical promiscuity on the part of bishops and priests by instituting clerical celibacy. We may not agree with his decision in the latter, but we also have no idea whether or not he intended celibacy to be in effect 1400 years later.

The second great transformation in the Church occurred in the eleventh Century when the Great

Schism occurred. The Orthodox Churches split from Rome primarily due to the East and the West having become so culturally dissimilar that they almost occupied different worlds. The proverbial straw that broke the camel's back was a disagreement over the filioque clause in the Nicene Creed. That clause states "I believe in the Holy Spirit, who proceeds from the Father and the Son." The Orthodox held that the clause should read, "I believe in the Holy Spirit, who proceeds from the Father," and in Orthodox churches to this day the Nicene Creed reads that way. Admittedly, to most contemporary believers that distinction is hard to get excited about, but in the eleventh century theologians became exercised enough about it to split the Church in two. What may be of more interest is that the Orthodox never accepted the doctrine of Original Sin, which posits essentially that humans are born guilty.

In looking at the third great transformation, I would argue that there were two parts to it. The first part was the reformation of the Carmelite Order by St. Teresa of Avila and St. John of the Cross, two Spanish Carmelite mystics who believed their Order had become too lax. Perhaps even more importantly, both St. John and St. Teresa wrote prolifically about the mystical life. Their writings continue to be central to understanding the mystical life today. Interestingly, they wrote during the sixteenth century, during the same years that the Reformation was gestating and coming to life.

What was the fourth great transformation? I believe we are in the early phase of the fourth great transformation right now. I say that because of the great influx of spiritual information from almost every tradition in the world, the concurrent decades long decline in church attendance, and a host of other reasons including the growing number of Christians who no longer find Atonement Theology, which claims that Jesus' death was a necessary sacrifice demanded of him by God to atone for our sins, to be an acceptable understanding of either Jesus or God. When the death of the concept of a corporeal, theistic God sitting on a throne just beyond the clouds is added to these factors it becomes clear that Christianity has to come to a new understanding of the life, mission, ministry, and death of Jesus. We now are working to bridge the gap into the future. To be able to bridge that gap effectively, we are going to have to redefine some concepts. Such a task is always threatening to some, and in the process of such sweeping reform any movement will lose some adherents. As our understandings of God grow, we need to find new ways to express those understandings in many different areas including our music, our worship forms, our theology, our sermons; even the names and labels that we choose to apply to our concepts. It is hard work, but it is absolutely essential to our being able to speak our truth clearly!

It is also interesting to note that other spiritual traditions had historic events take place around these times of Christian transformation. Approximately five hundred years before the birth of Christ the Jewish people were sent into exile and Buddha was born. At about the time of Pope Gregory's reforms, Muhammad was born. Right around the time of the Catholic-Orthodox schism, The Crusades were being fought against the Muslims. Could it be that there is something that all traditions share in common – the need for periodic reform – and if periodic reform does not occur then sooner or later more dramatic transformations occur?

9 WHO IS GOD?

We live in a world divided over God. In their arrogance and largely out of habit people of the Abrahamic faiths, who purport to believe that there is only one God, often find themselves at war with adherents of some other view of God. When Christians fight Muslims in a religiously based war, each tends to describe the other as Godless – without even pausing for a moment to consider that Christianity, Judaism, and Islam all have the same origins and so the same God! If we were logical *and* monotheistic, the worst that could happen would be that we would see people of other faiths as misguided. We could never see "their" God as a threat to "our" God because we wouldn't believe their God existed! What is really going on here?

It is my conviction that there is one God who is known by many different names and understood and worshiped in many different ways that are largely the result of the time and culture into which one is born and in which one is raised. At the risk of belaboring the obvious, it is important to note that such a God would be so vast and transcendent that all attempts to describe or define such a God would of necessity fall short, but in order to be able to talk about God we have to attempt some sort of definition.

What is God? That may seem a strange question, since most readers find the question, "Who is God?" to be more appropriate. In truth, both questions are appropriate, but we need to answer the first question before we can begin to attempt the second. Since we have to begin with some assumptions or our search would take an infinite number of volumes, let's begin with some traditional ones: God is all knowing, all seeing, all powerful, unchanging, all loving, eternal, and beyond or outside time. There are many more attributes that have traditionally been assigned to God, and our initial list does not imply that these are the only qualities. The list is a list which the vast majority of people willing to believe in God would be willing to affirm.

Is God corporeal? That is, does God have a physical body? Traditionally, God has been seen as an old white man with white hair and a long white beard who sits on a throne and lives just beyond the clouds in a place called heaven. I like to call that vision of God "Harold." As humanity developed the ability to fly above the clouds and even beyond our atmosphere one of the great questions in many Christians' mind was whether or not we would find God and/or heaven. A bit of history is in order at this point. In biblical times people conceived of the world as having three levels. You might think of it as a hamburger. The beef patty was the surface of the earth. The lower bun was called Sheol, the place where the dead went. It wasn't hell, it was more like nothingness. As Jewish thought developed, Sheol expanded to a two level affair called upper and lower Sheol. Lower Sheol was the place you didn't want to go because those who were there suffered the death of the body and the soul. In Upper Sheol one suffered only the death of the body. As Jewish thought began to entertain the possibility of the resurrection of the dead, only those from upper Sheol were eligible for resurrection. The top bun of the hamburger was the heavens, which contained everything in the sky and beyond.

The hamburger was understood to be the entirety of the universe. Everything that existed was somewhere within the hamburger. If God existed, God had to be somewhere within the hamburger. There was no concept of the universe beyond our atmosphere. Today, of course, we have a much greater understanding of astronomy, the planets, and the galaxy. God doesn't have to live anywhere we can locate, but that doesn't address the question of whether God has a body or not. Jesus himself gave us perhaps the biggest clue to the answer to this question when he said that, "God is spirit, and the time is coming and now is when true worshipers will worship God in spirit and truth." That seems to be a pretty comprehensive answer.

What about God's needs? Is God a being that needs anything? We have established that God doesn't have a physical body, which means that most of what we think of as needs cannot apply to God. Food, clothing, shelter, healthcare, and other physical needs don't apply. Some people believe that God has emotional needs - that God needs our worship, praise, prayer, and adoration. The short answer to this, despite what the Church has taught, is that God can't possibly need anything without ceasing to be God because to need is to change and we have defined God as being unchanging. Another consideration is that if God is really all powerful then God is by definition self sufficient. Finally, emotional needs are ego needs and egos are human problems, not divine problems.

We have established that God isn't in the heavens and that God doesn't have a body. We have also said that God doesn't have to "live" anywhere that we can locate, but we do need to know where to find God when we want to communicate with God. The major consideration is that, wherever we decide we can find God, it must be somewhere we can access. Since, with the rare exception of the accounts of those who claim they can travel at will outside their bodies and those who have near death experiences, most of us spend all of our lives inside our bodies, it must be true that God lives in us. I think it's important to say that God lives in everything and everybody, but for now let's concentrate on God living in us.

The God Within is a somewhat controversial notion in spirituality these days. Generally speaking it is a very helpful concept, but it is subject to misinterpretations that are not only inaccurate but potentially harmful. Given our starting point that there is one God known by many names, it may be obvious that THE God Within does not imply that this is one of many gods, but rather that this is one aspect of God - one place where God can be encountered. The God Within, then, implies neither that there are multiple gods nor the notion that I somehow AM the totality of God by virtue of God dwelling within me. After all, I dwell in my house but I would never assert that my house *is* me. I would more likely say that my house is one of the places in which I can be encountered - and so it is with God, who can be encountered within me (as well as any and everywhere else).

If God can be encountered any and everywhere, why is The God Within even worth mentioning? If God can be encountered anywhere, why is it necessary to point out that God can be encountered within *me*? First and foremost, if God dwells within me then I don't have to go to any physical place to find God. I may choose to go on pilgrimage or retreat (and those things are fine), but I don't have to. This also means that nobody can withhold God from me, because I already have God in me. The God Within has profound implications for prayer as well. I don't need to go anywhere to pray - to enter into dialogue with God or, even better, to enter into silence with God - because God is accessible to me at all times. A further advantage to having God within me is that I can feel free to pray in the place and in the way that feeds me most. While the notion of God Within is very helpful, distortions of it are potentially very damaging to a healthy spirituality. I believe there are two major distortions of the God Within. I call them the Ego Within and the Isolationist Within.

The Ego Within distortion fails to recognize that while God dwells within each of us, no one of us contains the totality of God. The Ego Within says, "I am God." The individual involved in this distortion believes that they have the mind of God. Ideas and spiritual practices that pop into this person's head are automatically and without prayer and reflection received as God's. You might say they go from reading tea leaves to reading toilet paper. This is not to say that God doesn't speak to people. It is to say that spiritually mature people who believe they are hearing from God tend to reveal what God is saying to them only after a period of prayer and reflection if at all. What's more, if the message they get from God is truly from God it will be consistent with the spiritual tradition of the individual receiving the message because that is the lens through which they will interpret the message. Stated plainly, God isn't going to tell anyone to jump off a bridge or blow up a clinic.

The Isolationist Within distorts the God Within into an excuse for spiritual withdrawal. As in the Ego Within, the Isolationist Within believes they contain the fullness of God within them. From this they conclude that they have need of nothing else. They either reject community worship or become members of small independent churches that have isolated themselves from the broader spiritual dialog. The problem with that is that such individuals and groups can easily drift into a belief system quite detached from reality without realizing it by virtue of the closed, almost inbred nature of their spiritual community. Any room into which fresh air is not allowed to flow becomes stale and musty very quickly. In the final analysis, a healthy understanding of the God Within requires that it pass the test of any healthy spiritual concept - it must be life giving, not life denying. Life giving things draw me out of myself, stretch me and move me out of my comfort zone and into a fuller encounter with life and with God. Anything less is life denying and cannot possibly be of God.

How does God act in the world? The answer is through you and me, led by the indwelling Holy Spirit. Inside of all humanity, born into all of us, are stirrings and leadings and the knowledge of right and wrong, fairness and justice, compassion and love - all of which influence how we act on the world. Whatever name you wish to attribute to these motivations, for the purposes of our discussion here we will call them the indwelling of the Spirit. When we act according to these influences, these actions are in fact God at work. This can be clearly seen by the altruistic, life giving actions that spring from these motivations. You might say, with the folks from New Thought and others, God works in us, through us, and as us!

Of course there are motivations that do not spring from the influence of Holy Mother Wisdom. Left to our own devices we can and do act selfishly, tribally, and to the detriment of others – but the Spirit moves us otherwise. If you doubt this reality, all you have to do is watch the evening news or look to the massive amounts of negative karma that all of us have accumulated. We can also look to the horrifying actions of the early Hebrew people, who assumed they were acting in accord with God's will as they wiped out towns, cities, villages, and kingdoms while raping, burning, and pillaging. They did not understand the truth that God lives within everything and everybody because Sophia/Wisdom/Spirit had not yet arisen in them, and so they acted only from the natural law of survival of the fittest. Perhaps the most important part of Jesus' message and mission was to finally put an end to the Law by fulfilling it and replacing it demonstratively with the sending of the Holy Spirit. The Law was no longer the measurement of one's walk with God, the indwelling Spirit and the new Law of Love was and is. In fact, if we ever become successful at living by the Law of Love, all other Laws will shrivel and die of their own accord.

How do we know when God is present in our decisions and our choices? We can ask ourselves the critically important question, "Where is God in this for me?" That may seem like a strange question, but in the final analysis it is the most important question of our lives. You can feel free to substitute whatever word you are most comfortable with for the word "God" in that question - Allah, Great Spirit, the Divine, the Transcendent, the Universe, or any other. The question remains the most important question we could ever ask - and the most necessary. Most of us don't ask that question often enough, and I believe we don't ask it because it takes a fair amount of time to ask the question and to wait for our answer.

We need to ask the question because it provides a balance to our ego, which constantly screams for attention and seeks to direct our lives. When I hear people talking about life decisions and life changes only in the context of what *they* want I become very concerned because the perspective of the individual is very limited indeed, and psychologically tends to be completely self interested. Not unlike a toddler grabbing things and screaming "MINE!" the ego tends to reject anything that is the least bit uncomfortable or that stretches us into growing in any way. Asking where God is in all of this forces us to listen to another perspective - and that perspective is always broader than our own.

Some of you are skeptical at this point, and I can't blame you. We have all seen examples of people who have projected their own hare-brained ideas onto God and announced that God told them to do something stupid. There are some guidelines to follow to guard against this kind of abuse of power. The first is that God is not a computer. You don't simply ask God a question and get an immediate response as if God were sitting on the edge of a chair just waiting for you to ask your question. God speaks to us through the still, small voice within, and hearing that voice is a process that requires discernment, not a task calling for haste. The interesting thing about a process is that it requires frequent attention. One doesn't run around in an active frenzy never taking time to listen to that still small voice within and then expect it to suddenly provide an answer on demand.

When the first opportunity arose to take a teenager who had no place to go into our home that still small voice within asked me a question. The question was, "You talk a good game, but can you practice what you preach?" That question didn't come out of the dark. It was the fruit of a process of self examination and reflection. The second, third, and fourth time we were confronted with the same question I already knew where God was in this - God was in the child at the door.

In my work in the Church and society I frequently encounter people who are absorbed with "My, Me, and Mine." They talk about *my* ministry, what's best for *me*, and the things they have accomplished with a sense of possessiveness - *mine.* In reality, nothing except my body and what is discharged from it are *mine,* and my body is a temporary possession. Even the things we create, once they are finished and made public, are no longer ours. Why then would we look at the world around us and act on it as if we owned it?

Why? I suggest it is because we don't know where God is in all of this, or because we are too fear based to let go of anything to anyone - even God. From our fear comes a need to control, and from control comes a need to squash everything that frightens us. Frankly, Scarlett, we don't give a damn where God is because God *always* calls us out of ourselves into a broader perspective and *that* scares the hell out of us.

Here's the news flash - you came into this world naked and you will go out of it in the same condition. All the "my, me, and mine" in the world won't change that one bit. What remains after we are gone are those moments when we stepped into the places where we find God active and present in every corner of our lives *and act in a way that is informed by that presence.* All the rest is self deception. Every argument, every moment spent arguing or (worse) fighting about anything is a moment lost. If we cannot learn to live with uncertainty about how the world works we will continue to construct complicated denials of reality and seek comfort in those fictions of our own creation. If we finally don't realize that the Universe is so infinitely vast that we will never know everything there is to know and so must learn to be content with an understanding and belief system that we hold loosely we will waste our lives in search of something we can never find and live in fear of what comes next. Most importantly, if we don't learn to allow others to have their own view of God and not feel compelled to try to convert them to our view of God, we will destroy our planet in the name of the God many believe created it.

10 SPIRITUALITY AND SCIENCE

If we are trying to understand who we are we need to start by looking at our origins. In contemporary America we have seen the development of pseudo-science that seeks to justify the biblical, pre-scientific world view. The Bible says that the world was created in seven days, even though there wasn't a sun until the third day. We simply cannot attempt to understand that story literally while at the same time speaking credibly with people who have even a passing acquaintance with science. On the other hand, there is nothing about the Genesis story understood as metaphor that prohibits SBNR people from holding to the Big Bang theory of creation and believing that what we call God is and was the energy not only behind the Big Bang but also the energy that supports and sustains all that is, was, and ever will be. We *aren't* saying that an embodied God made everything. We *are* saying that whatever that energy was, it has to be included in our understanding of Divinity. When the time comes that science develops a more concise theory than the Big Bang, we can with integrity hold that theory.

What of the biblical creation narrative? It is a wonderful folk tale that was created in response to the question, "Mommy and Daddy, where did we come from?" That story to contain many truths in the form of metaphor, but to believe it to be a literal, historical, or scientific account of creation is to abandon all reason and intellect in service to a flawed tradition. There are, after all, actually two accounts of creation in the Book of Genesis that differ in significant ways. In addition to the previously mentioned problem that the sun doesn't appear until the third "day" of creation, there are other problems. These include the patriarchy and oppression that has resulted from the biblical account of woman being taken from man, created from a rib of his, and named by man along with the animals and subsequently being responsible for the fall of humankind from the Garden of Eden; the Flood in which all living things perished except those aboard Noah's Ark and wherein the entire world was seen to be covered with water is not a scientific possibility, nor is the notion of God committing genocide very attractive; the three tiered view of the world including the flat earth theory; and there are many others. Biblical literalists of all stripes have gone to great effort to explain these things away, but we must ask what kind of an all-powerful God would need human beings to explain away "facts" about the creation?

From this we can see that "creation science" is a complete and total fiction, and that the so-called scientists who support it are no longer scientist but rather apologists for the flat earth society. One of the saddest moments in my personal experience came when I read that my Alma Mater, Wisconsin Lutheran College, had established a creation science program. When I attended Wisconsin Lutheran College it was a school with great intellectual integrity. Those days are obviously gone, as is any chance of my financially supporting that institution.

As spiritual people, we can agree with the Dalai Lama that if and when science proves that something we believe is not correct, we must change what we believe. We hold that scientists perform the very worthwhile job of investigating the universe of which

God is the Ground of Being. In doing so, they cannot help but teach us about God. We need to listen. Of course, we need to listen with a discerning mind, for science is not perfect and is subject to error just as any field of human endeavor is prone to error. The key is to remain fluid in thought and belief, and to avoid at all costs becoming entrenched in yesterday's truth. The only way science can threaten our beliefs is if we have made our belief system dependent on a literally true Bible or other ancient document that was never written or intended to be literally true.

It seems that one day our universe will end. The resulting implosion will no doubt impact our galaxy. It is foolish to assume that we are the only living beings in a constantly expanding universe, and it is equally foolish to scan the skies for UFOs. When the universe comes to an end it will not do so in the way that the Book of Revelation predicts. The Book of Revelation is a highly symbolic piece of literature that belongs to the genre of Jewish Apocalyptic literature. It has never been appropriate to take that literature literally, just as no thinking, rational person would hop into an oven after reading the Book of Daniel (another example of Jewish Apocalyptic literature).

Medicine, as a part of science, is a vital part of any responsible spirituality. We must reject as ignorant and irresponsible any parent who would deny their child medical treatment for any reason. We also must find religious beliefs and systems that would deny medical treatment to anyone for any reason to be sinful and primitive. Even as we affirm the value and effectiveness of prayer, we cannot responsibly believe it should ever take the place of medical care. Prayer, which should understood primarily as an exchange of energy rather than beseeching a non-existent interventionist Deity to act, and medicine are two complementary but distinct fields. We need both.

Remember the Washington D.C area snipers, Lee Boyd Malvo and John Allen Muhammad? I will never forget hearing a young woman interviewed on CNN thanking God for making her late so that she missed her bus the day that Lee Malvo and John Muhammad attacked that same bus. "God was watching over me!" she claimed. This story illustrates well the problem with the belief in an interventionist God. If God was watching over her, God was also apparently choosing to allow a bus filled with people to come under attack. That belief posits a God who is, quite frankly, inattentive, abusive, incompetent, capricious, and irresponsible. If that is how God acts, I want nothing to do with God.

In the biblical creation story we learn that we have been made custodians of the created order. This means that environmentalism should be a part of our spirituality. Since God is the Source of All, including nature, those who claim to believe in God simply *must* be concerned for all of creation. We must recognize that to destroy the environment is to destroy ourselves, our children and grandchildren. As part of our stewardship of creation, we must have absolute respect for all living beings – humans, plants, and animals – as well as inanimate parts of creation such as natural resources. The primary evidence for this goodness is the Incarnation of Christ.

The Incarnation is one of the four pivotal events for followers of Jesus (the others are the Crucifixion,

Resurrection, and Ascension), and it is important to clarify the meaning of the Incarnation. The Incarnation holds that God became human in Jesus. When we say God became human, as opposed to God became man, we mean that God became present in all of humanity, not just in the one person Jesus. In fact, God has been present in everyone and everything since before time began. The Incarnation was an undeniable demonstration and reminder of that truth. In the Incarnation, the created order was definitively shown to be good – completely good – because God is part and source of the entire creation. God has never seen the created order to be bad. The belief that God understood the creation to be bad was a distortion that occurred when the story of the Garden of Eden was taken to be a literal, historical account and Greco-Roman philosophy was applied to it – most notably so-called Original Sin. Most likely in order to induce guilt, we were taught that although we were created in the image and likeness of God, we lost either the likeness and/or the image of God in the Fall of Adam and Eve. Nothing could be farther from the truth.

The story of creation tells us that when God created all that is God saw it all to be good. We believe that God is all seeing and all knowing – that has always been part of the definition of God – and that God exists outside of time. That is to say that all moments are the present moment to God. This truth about the timelessness of God has been held throughout all of Christian history. What this means is that to God the moment of creation, the moment of the alleged Fall and the moment you read this are the same moment. If God sees all and knows all, how can creation possibly be both all good and also bad/fallen/evil at the same time? It is contradictory for both of these things to be true at the same time.

So what? The Incarnation is what. The Incarnation is God's definitive statement that the created order is wholly and totally good. That truth is re-affirmed every time a child is born, because all children are born totally and wholly good – without stain of any kind, except perhaps in its diaper. You may be thinking that this is all great, but if it is just a theological position that one holds why should I be interested? The answer is that how you view humanity and the created order has a lot to do with how you make ethical decisions. If the created order is good, then environmental concerns are not only appropriate but essential. The Earth cannot possibly exist to be plundered and destroyed. If all human beings are good, then none of us can stand by and watch other human beings starve or have substandard health care – *anywhere* in the world. Equally important, we cannot allow human beings to be exploited in any way – not by the sex slave trade, not by substandard wages or working conditions, not by the evils of racism and tribalism, or in any other way. May we all be constantly reminded of the goodness of all that is, and may we also be led to act in accord with that goodness to protect *all* of creation: humanity, the animal kingdom, and the environment – both on the Earth and beyond it. It's not only practical, it's imperative for our very survival as a species and a planet.

Before I conclude this chapter, since I mentioned Original Sin it is important to discuss that odd doctrine since it has had such a profoundly distorted impact on how we understand our relationship with God. Original Sin is the brainchild of a man known to us as St. Augustine. It was never accepted in Orthodox Christianity. To be sure, St. Augustine had quite a few important spiritual insights and should not be remembered primarily for Original Sin. However, prior to being ordained against his will (a curious thing that happened in the early Church), St. Augustine had a little problem with his pants. It seems they kept falling off in the presence of women, and rather than simply pull his pants up he felt compelled to do a mattress dance first. Then he found himself on the way to being consecrated bishop and he had to deal with his rather unsavory escapades. He looked to the scriptures and said, "I'm not a man-ho, I'm just a victim of Original Sin!" Everybody said, "What's Original Sin?" And slick old Augustine said, "It makes your pants fall down!" Suddenly babies were born with "the stain of original sin," and baptism was supposed to cleanse them from that stain. I've changed a fair number of diapers and can tell you the only stain I have ever seen on a baby is in those diapers.

In the Gospels Jesus encounters a man born blind and Jesus' disciples ask, "Who sinned that this man was born blind – him or his parents?" Jesus replied, "No one sinned." Did you catch that? No one sinned – not, Adam sinned, or it was because of Original Sin, but just plain old, "No one sinned." Why is that important? It's important because every person – the good, the bad, the ugly, and everyone in between – is born perfect good and sinless. Yes, that means you.

Institutional Christianity, except the Eastern Orthodox, grabbed on to the whole Original Sin/Original Guilt thing and has been squeezing people by their coin purses ever since. It's time we reject the idea of Original Sin causing us to be born guilty, that the belief is a practice of extortion, and it needs to stop. Do we sin? We absolutely do sin. When we hurt one another or act in ways that are lacking in compassion we sin. Is there an "original sin?" If there is it is probably something like trying to get ahead at the expense of others, but that is a learned behavior and not one we are born with. You don't see babies trying to get ahead at the expense of other babies. Can we stop sinning? We absolutely can. It will be a process, and it won't happen overnight, but as we move toward enlightenment and becoming a fully integrated human being, we will sin less and less. It is perfectly okay to be you, and you are perfectly okay – even with your imperfections! Now that IS good news!

Why all of this concern about Original Sin and sin in general? The concern is present because how we understand the mistakes we make and whether or not we believe we came into this world as good, complete human beings will have a profound impact on our understanding of our relationship with God, not to mention our self esteem. Some years ago at a conference in America, the Dalai Lama was asked a question about poor self esteem. He didn't understand the term, and so he turned to his translator for the word in Tibetan that meant low self esteem. Such a word doesn't exist in the Tibetan language. When the concept was explained to the Dalai Lama, he was mystified as to why anybody would feel badly about themselves! He was mystified because Buddhists believe that all of humanity carries within it what they call Buddha

Nature. They believe that Buddha Nature gets obscured by the events of day to day living, but that doesn't change that within each of us is a Buddha, waiting to be uncovered.

An authentic understanding of the Incarnation leads us to see that within each of us there is what we variously call "Buddha Nature," "Christ Nature," "God Nature," or "God Consciousness," or, more directly, "God." We have already established that the Incarnation of God as humanity in Jesus Christ signaled that the entire creation is good, not bad. We also said that God has no body but ours, that we are God's hands and feet, that God dwells within us, and that God lives and works in us, through us, and as us. How could this possibly be if we were inherently or innately sinful?

Worse than Original Sin, but related to it, is the understanding in some Protestant circles of the total depravity of humanity. These folks argue that when Eve ate the apple, causing her and Adam to be expelled from the Garden of Eden, they lost both the image *and* the likeness of God. That means that not a trace of God could be found in humanity after the Fall. Humanity was (and is, they believe) totally depraved and without an ounce of goodness to be found in any person. We can't possibly hope to grow, we can't make any sort of spiritual progress, we certainly can't draw closer to God – all we can possibly hope for is to not dig the hole any deeper. Can you imagine a more depressing notion? I certainly can't, and I also believe such a concept denies that God became human in Christ and that God lives in us now. Such concepts were, not surprisingly, pretty effective at keeping people coming to church and emptying their wallets in the collection plate. They were also lies told in the name of God that used a false, Church-created fear of a wrathful, judgmental, punishing God (another fiction created by the Church) and as such are inherently evil done in the name of God. These kinds of images, both of humanity and God, have been responsible for more than a few people leaving the institutional Church – and with good reason. They are unhealthy perspectives, and a mature spirituality requires a healthy understanding of the God-human relationship!

11 WHO IS JESUS?

For much of the Christian world, the question contained in the title of this chapter is completely off limits. There is only one acceptable answer, and that answer is found in the Nicene and Apostles Creed. It's also found in a more cumbersome and rather redundant document called the Athanasian Creed. For sake of simplicity, we will examine the Nicene Creed here:

The Nicene Creed

We believe in one God,
the Father, the Almighty,
maker of heaven and earth,
of all that is, seen and unseen.

We believe in one Lord, Jesus Christ,
the only Son of God,
eternally begotten of the Father,
God from God, Light from Light,
true God from true God,
begotten, not made,

of one Being with the Father.

Through him all things were made.

For us and for our salvation

he came down from heaven:

by the power of the Holy Spirit

he became incarnate from the Virgin Mary,

and was made man.

For our sake he was crucified under Pontius Pilate;

he suffered death and was buried.

On the third day he rose again

in accordance with the Scriptures;

he ascended into heaven

and is seated at the right hand of the Father.

He will come again in glory to judge the living and the dead,

and his kingdom will have no end.

We believe in the Holy Spirit, the Lord, the giver of life,

who proceeds from the Father and the Son.

With the Father and the Son he is worshiped and glorified.

He has spoken through the Prophets.

We believe in one holy catholic and apostolic Church.

We acknowledge one baptism for the forgiveness of sins.

We look for the resurrection of the dead,

and the life of the world to come. Amen.

For most of Christianity, that's all you need to know and believe, but you must know and believe all of it, despite the fact that a good deal of the language isn't very clear to contemporary people who were raised outside the Church. Those good people have many questions when they read this Creed.

Jesus is the only son of God? I thought we all were children of God. Begotten, not made? What is begotten? Jesus came down from heaven. Where, exactly, is that? He "became incarnate" from the Virgin Mary by the power of the Holy Spirit. A virgin, pregnant from a Spirit, who by definition is without penis or sperm? How, precisely, does that happen, and what does the fact that it happened mean for us? He was made [hu]man. How was that done? If he was eternally begotten, when was he made human? Why? For our sake he was crucified. For our sake? I thought he got arrested in the Garden, and I wasn't even born yet! How was that for my sake? On the third day he rose again...ascended into heaven. How did this happen? How exactly did he get to heaven, and where is it? Why did he go back there? He will come again in glory. How will he come again? Is there a shuttle from heaven to earth?

These are but a few of the questions that those unfamiliar with Church-speak have upon their first exposure to the Creed. We could look at the longer Athanasian Creed and the shorter Apostles Creed and be just as confused. To someone who has not been raised in the Church, these documents raise more questions than they answer. They ask us to believe some pretty incredible things that, to most people, just don't make much sense and seem very unlikely. How can contemporary, uninitiated people come to understand this Jesus? A sarcastic poster sums the problem up very well when it says:

Christianity: The belief that a cosmic Jewish Zombie who was his own father can make you live forever if you symbolically eat his flesh and telepathically tell him you accept him as your master, so he can remove an evil force from your soul that is present in humanity

because a rib-woman was convinced by
a talking snake to eat from a magical tree...
yeah, makes perfect sense.

At the time of Jesus' birth, just about every important person was said to be born of a virgin. I, too, was born of a virgin – at least to hear my father tell it, but I digress. The Roman Emperor was born of a Virgin, Kings and Pharaohs were born of virgins. You might think that in ancient times you couldn't swing a dead cat without hitting a pregnant virgin. The truth is the being born of a virgin was a literary device used to indicate that someone was very important, indeed. You see, the Virgin Mary, isn't - at least not if we understand virginity to be about an intact hymen. (I do believe that every traditional Christian doctrine that seems incredible can be understood as true if we abandon literalism and even historical criticism and examine them non-dually, but that is beyond the scope of this book.)

Have you ever been in a labor and delivery room? If you haven't, check it out on the Discovery Health

Channel. This will be a newsflash to some of my conservative friends, but no baby gets born with a hymen still intact. I have heard there are occasional exceptions, but those stories are anecdotal. Certainly, Jesus' brothers and sisters knocked that hymen out if Jesus somehow didn't get all of it. What's more, that hymen wasn't even there when Jesus came out because Joseph took care of it at the conception. That's not scandalous, it's simple biology.

How can I say that? I say that because babies need two things to get born - sperm and an egg. Back in biblical days, before in-vitro fertilization, they needed a penis and a uterus together, in the same room – actually, much closer than that – to have a baby. Miracles may happen, but when they do happen they do not represent disruption of the laws of nature or requirements of biology. What's more, God is Spirit and so is the Holy Spirit (it's right there in her name, "Holy Spirit") and so neither of them has genitals. Despite all the very disturbing debates about this over the ages, there ain't no Holy Penis except Joseph's.

But how can Jesus be God's Son if there isn't a

Holy Penis? The same way that you and I are children of God: through the sanctifying grace of the Holy Spirit and by opening himself radically to love and grace and compassion. If you think a Holy Penis is stronger than those things, we need to talk about your preoccupation with Divine Genitalia.

Mary isn't and wasn't a physical virgin because Jesus, to be fully human, had to (1) be born of a man and a woman, (2) needed a mother who was a human mother, not some sexless vision of a sick, patriarchal society in which women were desired sexually by men but then blamed for the man's desire once the act was over. He didn't need "divine blood lines" to be divine. That notion comes from a pre scientific, Jewish lens that had great value attached to the first born male that we post modern people couldn't care less about.

Do you really want Mary to be a life long celibate and to be used to oppress women as she has been? Can you even begin to relate to a woman who supposedly loves her husband but loves God more and so "saves herself for God"? Would that not reflect a profoundly psychotic process at work? Why would God care about a hymen? Can you fathom why Joseph would have even married such a nut case? How emasculated would he had to have been? Do you really want the disgusting, allegedly celibate, sexual cripples that are the historic Roman Catholic Magisterium to define what is and isn't appropriate sexual behavior for a woman, especially given the legend of clerical celibacy that insists that those same individuals have never seen a grown woman naked (except, perhaps, their housekeeper)? Do you really think that you are going to get away with telling me that my wife, whom I love more intensely than you can imagine, is somehow less a human being because we have a truly intimate, adult relationship that has a sexual component? What about your mother? Was she a whore because she had sex with your Father? Would she have been better off "consecrating her virginity to God?"

Let's be honest for a change. Mary's alleged virginity was the stuff of legend in biblical times - legends that were told to signify that a birth was important. Kings were born of virgins, emperors were born of virgins - the list goes on and on. What's more, the birth narratives were the last things added to the Gospels and only appear in two of them. There was a time when this particular piece of mythological language served a purpose, but that day has long passed and we need to dismiss it in the same way we have dismissed biblical visions of a flat earth supported by four pillars.

Let's instead recognize Mary as a model for real women. The Bible tells us that Mary, concerned that Jesus had gone a bit off his rocker, showed up at a home where he was teaching seeking to take him home before he got himself in trouble. That's real parental instinct, something a real mother would do. Mary stood at the foot of the cross, weeping as her son died, and he commended her to the care of St. John. That's something a real, loving son would do for his real, loving mother. She changed his diapers, he ate from her breast.

It's hard to believe that some people are really sick enough to believe that a hymen has anything to do with any of it. Do I seem angry? You bet I am! I am angry for two thousand years of the persecution of women through the imposition of this "ideal" of womanhood that has been foisted upon people in the Name of God by an institutional Church that has committed perhaps its greatest sin in doing so. I mourn for all women who have been adversely affected by this nonsense, who have felt guilt about being a sexual being because of Church teachings such as Mary's virginity that are life-denying. It simply has to stop, and the only was it is going to stop is for both men and women to reject it for the abusive nonsense it is.

Once we are freed from this life denying, mythological view of the Virgin Birth, we can – if we choose to – still understand Mary as a type of virgin. Rather than being the type of virgin the Church has historically made her out to be – a virgin who says that female sexuality is bad and somehow dirty – we can talk about her virginity as being a metaphor for her openness and receptivity to the Holy Spirit. We can see her as a woman of great spiritual depth, not some lunatic who was visited by an angel, conceived a child without sexual contact, but then some years later (according to the Gospels) went to retrieve Jesus from a house where he was preaching, thinking he had lost his mind. Wouldn't a woman who had been told by the Holy Spirit that her child was going to be of great religious significance expect that he would be preaching some pretty outrageous things? Why would she take her other children to assist her in retrieving Jesus? Hadn't the family at some point shared the identity of Jesus with one another as they sat around the fire?

Of course they didn't, and the reason they didn't is that the birth narratives were mythological stories that were written seventy to eighty years after the birth of Jesus and never intended to be taken as literal accounts of his birth. There wouldn't have been any records or accounts of yet another poor child born to poor parents in a one donkey town in rural Israel. They are beautiful mythological stories that lose their beauty and become horrible instruments of oppression when we literalize them – as so much of the Bible does when we literalize it! When we understand them as beautiful stories of a very special birth that use the symbolic language of the time to relay a story that is true, even though it didn't happen the way it is written, we can reclaim the scriptures and take women off of the hook their hymen has been hanging on for the last two thousand years. Now, that is a beautiful thing!

This necessarily leads us to another interesting question about Jesus. Did he pop out of the womb with a complete understanding of his identity and mission, or did he have an evolving understanding of his identity and mission? Did he reach up with his little, newborn fingers, wipe away the afterbirth and coo. "I am the Son of God," after which he promptly pooped? Traditional Christian understanding has favored the idea that Jesus popped out fully aware of his identity and mission. There are even legends about Jesus resuscitating a dead bird and making another bird out of mud and breathing life into it. Surely these are the stuff of fancy and legend.

Let's return to the question of Mary showing up with Jesus' siblings to take his crazy self home. If Jesus knew he was the Messiah, wouldn't he just have stepped out of the room and spoken with his mother, saying, "Mom, I told you, I am the Christ, for Christ's sake!!!!!" and wouldn't she have believed him? Instead, the overwhelming Gospel evidence is that Jesus denied that he was Divine! Only in John's Gospel, the latest written and most theologically processed, is Jesus made to accept claims of divinity laid upon him.

Can you imagine the consequences of a teenage Jesus that knew he was the Messiah? Could anything have been more obnoxious? I know that the notion of an obnoxious teen Jesus is blasphemy to some people, but we have to be able to ask these questions if we are to take Jesus seriously because these are the questions those raised outside of religion are asking! Did Jesus, as a thirteen year old boy do what most thirteen year old boys have done – discover his penis? What kind of divinity can't stand up to questions?

Last but not least, a Jesus who fully understood his mission and identity from the beginning would have been play acting on the cross. If he knew that everything was going to be fine, that he would be raised on the third day, the only struggle on the cross would have been physical pain. There would have been no need for anguish, no need to cry out, "My God, My

God, why have you forsaken me?" had he known that he was not, in fact, forsaken but would be raised on the third day. Jesus may well have had hints of who he was but those hints would have come through an evolving sense of his mission and identity. Jesus went to the cross believing for all the world that he was going to die and that was the end of it but also having faith in God to work everything our – and that is the beauty and power of the story, because he went to the cross not as some sort of bizarre blood atonement for our sins as we have been taught, but rather because he loved so radically and stood so powerfully for the marginalized that he was a threat to the power structures of his day and they killed him for it. That is the message of Jesus, the truly Good News that in Jesus God cared enough for the downtrodden to die for them – and left us an example to follow. The message is love, not virginity. Perhaps those who cling the hardest to the myth of Mary's perpetual virginity are those who most struggle to love.

So, then, if Jesus isn't born of a virgin and if the Holy Spirit wasn't his biological father, what made and makes him special? Was he just another teacher? Clearly he was more than just another teacher, because the run of the mill teacher of Jesus' day is not remembered today. Was he Divine? Absolutely, but so are you and I bearers of and sharers in Divinity. What made Jesus able to do the things he did and teach so effectively was that he radically opened himself to God and so was infused with God Consciousness in a unique but not exclusive way. By that I mean that Jesus was not the only person in history to be radically infused with God Consciousness – all of the great, enduring spiritual and religious teachers have been so infused, even those who manifested on Earth before Jesus. After all, didn't Abraham and Moses walk with God? So did the Old Testament prophets, as well as Muhammad, Krishna, the Buddhas, and all the founders of all the great, enduring religious and spiritual traditions. Best of all, so can you and I!

It's important for me to clarify why I prefer the term God Consciousness to the more often used "Christ Consciousness." One of the definitions of Christ Consciousness is "...a grown up version of belief in which God is a true parent, teaching God's children what they need and turning them loose to make mistakes, perhaps suffer injury, but in the end to mature and transform." I think that is an excellent definition of God Consciousness, and I am more comfortable calling it God Consciousness that Christ Consciousness for two reasons. The first is that what we believe in is God's action, not Christ's. The second, and more important reason, is that we are living into an age of pluralism. The very term Christ Consciousness is way too Christo-centric for me. Recall that we said in chapter four that there is one God known by many different names. As we seek to develop a mature spirituality that transcends tribalism, it makes no sense to approach Muslims, for example, and say to them that Muhammad had Christ Consciousness. Imagine how the average Christian would react to being told that Jesus had Muhammad Consciousness! Since 2008 I have been teaching that we need to attribute the Consciousness we find in the Christ and in all the great spiritual masters to the Source of All – God. I realize that this flies in the face of the developing tradition around Christ Consciousness and I mean no disrespect to those who teach Christ Consciousness, but if we are to move to the place where we can speak of this new vision of God to people from all traditions, to a truly interspiritual perspective, I believe we have to call it what it is – God Consciousness.

It was God Consciousness that provided Jesus with the wisdom and the vision the powered his teaching and his healing. It was that same God Consciousness that people could see shining forth from him that caused them to quite literally drop what they were doing and follow him. The full, deep, rich, and powerful presence of God within Jesus drove him to work for the inclusion of the marginalized of his day and gave him the strength to love so radically that his society recognized they could not control him – and so they killed him. Finally, it was God Consciousness that raised Jesus from the grave and allowed him to appear to his followers to inspire them to carry for the message that Jesus had taught. That message was that we are all inseparably connected to God, and that each of us can do the very things that Jesus did and more if we open ourselves to that same God Consciousness. What a radically transformative concept!

12 NONSECTARIAN INTERSPIRITUAL TEACHINGS

A large part of my spiritual journey over the last few years has been articulating a nonsectarian interspiritual practice. This means that the primary spiritual teachings I articulate are shared by a variety of spiritual traditions. Another way to look at these teachings is that they are among the teachings that the largest, most enduring spiritual traditions hold in common and to which they attach high value. In this chapter we examine a few such teachings.

Mindfulness and the Present Moment

Buddhism, Hinduism, and some contemporary "spiritual teachers" who like to plagiarize from the historic traditions without quoting their sources teach that the only moment in which we can live is the present moment. Yesterday is gone and will not return, tomorrow has not arrived yet and so we cannot influence it. In fact, the only time in which we live is now. When tomorrow gets here, it will be now, too.

Despite these truths, many of us daydream our lives away and have only periodic, almost accidental, contact with the present moment.

Have you ever driven your car home from somewhere and when you arrived not been certain how you got there? It is a frightening experience that most of us have had at one time or another. In fact, it is a very dangerous experience because it means that while we were driving our fifteen hundred to three thousand pound vehicles down the road we were not paying attention! We were mentally off somewhere else, perhaps day dreaming, perhaps worrying about some problem we were having or reliving some conversation we wished we had handled better. Whatever was occupying our minds, it was the last thing we should have been paying attention to while we were driving, and yet for many of us this kind of thing is a regular occurrence!

It amazes me every time I watch my daughter wash dishes. I don't mean to pick on her, I see the same thing from her friends. She washes dishes with one of her shoulders lifted high and pressing her cell phone to her ear. Part of me admires her flexibility, and how seldom she drops her phone into the dishwater – which does happen, just not nearly as often as it would happen to me if I tried to do the same thing. I also have to confess that there are times when I listen to music while doing dishes, so I am not exempt from voluntary distractions, either. One way to measure how out of the present moment the person washing dishes really was is to examine the allegedly clean dishes. If carrying on a phone conversation makes a relatively simple task like washing dishes successfully rather difficult, imagine the impact is has on our ability to drive a car!

The truth is that the present moment is all we have. Thich Nhat Hanh reminds us that it we don't dwell in the present moment we could very well live our life and reach the end of it never really having lived, all of our time having been spent in the past or the future. I recommend trying the following experiment. The next time you have to drive somewhere, leave the radio or CD player in your car turned off. If you're like me, you'll discover how much more focused and peaceful you are when you arrive at your destination. I'm not advocating taking the radio or CD player out of your car, There are times when it can be very nice to take a drive listening to your favorite music or an audio book. You may just find that, after trying the experiment in your car, you want to try it in your living room. I strongly suggest you try the experiment the next time you have a conversation with someone you care about. If you are really present to them, without the usual distractions, you might actually hear each other!

The Golden Rule

Do unto others as you would have them do unto you. Interestingly, the Christian formula of the Golden Rule is the only one that states it positively. In other traditions it is stated, "Do not do unto others what you would not have them do unto you." The positive formulation is actually more demanding. It's not enough to avoid doing something wrong to someone else, people are required to focus on doing the right thing, to actually acting instead of simply avoiding action. If you see someone in a situation and recognize that if you were in that same situation you would appreciate some help, you are required to act. Over the years, people have justified all kinds of poor behavior by being less than forthcoming about what they would like done to them. Imagine the likelihood of someone actually believing, "If that were me, I'd want to be excommunicated!"

Love Your Neighbor as Yourself

One of the two Great Commandments of Jesus, Love Your Neighbor as Yourself, is also more observed in its absence. Like the Golden Rule, much of the problem lies in people being less than forthcoming about how one responds in love. I have actually heard pastors say that excommunication is loving!

For Westerners in particular, some of the struggle with this commandment is that we don't love ourselves very much. Some of that is related to poor self esteem and a culture of conditional love. Many of us were raised in environments of very conditional love or, worse yet, abuse. Compounding the problem are Churches who have taught that healthy self esteem and self love are equivalent to sinful pride! Our culture has been reaping the rewards of those approaches in the form of widespread depression and other mental health issues for decades. I believe these factors also contribute to our high divorce rate. I simply have to love myself to be able to love you. We need to remind people that the very God of the Universe dwells within them, and in each and every human being as well as every other living thing. All of us are wonderful just as we are, perfect in our imperfection, and getting better all the time. A large part of loving our neighbor is found in reminding each other of this truth!

Compassion

Compassion is part of loving our neighbor, but bears discussion on its own. Love and compassion are the heart of every spiritual or religious system. You won't find an authentic spirituality that preaches hate and coldheartedness! Compassion is more than an attitude, it is a practice. Like any spiritual practice, it needs to be developed. One of the most effective ways that I know to develop increased compassion is found in a loving kindness practice I learned from Buddhist teacher Sharon Salzberg.

To engage in this practice, find a quiet place where you won't be interrupted. Turn off your phone, computer, pager, and anything else that might interrupt you. Sit comfortably in a chair with your feet flat on the floor and your hands either on your lap or on your knees. If you have back problems that make sitting problematic, feel free to lay down on the floor or in your bed, but try to stay awake. Take a few minutes to allow your thought s to settle. Starting with yourself, speak silently the words, "May I be happy, may I be healthy, may I be safe, may I live at ease." Repeat those words several times, and when you are ready think of someone you love and silently say, "May they be happy, may they be healthy, may they be safe, may they live at ease." If it helps, say the person's name instead of "they." Repeat that process several times. Then, when you feel ready, say the words for someone you feel neutral about. After that move on to someone who irritates you. Move on to the person with whom you have the most difficulty. Conclude by saying the words for every living being on the planet.

If you engage in this practice on a regular basis – preferably daily, but at least three times a week – you will be amazed at the changes you see in yourself in just a few months. You will respond to other people in a much more compassionate way. Another practice that is very helpful in developing a more level response to the events of daily life is meditation and/or mantra practice. There are many ways to meditate, and literally hundreds of books available on the subject.

Attachment and Materialism

In truth, attachment and materialism are closely related, because without attachment materialism could not exist. We can become attached to much more than things, however. We can become attached to people, places, entertainment, activities, even rituals and religious observances. What is attachment? Attachment is essentially the belief that a person, place, or thing will always exist just as it is today and it must remain that way for me to continue to exist. It rapidly transforms into a *need* for that person place or thing to always exist just as it is today. My new car must never get a scratch, my favorite coffee cup must never break, I must be eternally young, and you must always love me (and never change or age), are but a few of the myriad examples of attachment, which is based on the denial of the spiritual and physical reality that everything changes.

Many people whose parents, grandparents, or great grandparents lived through the great depression were raised in households replete with attachment. It was understandable, because in those days of economic crisis it was often very true that if something broke people couldn't afford to replace it. My own grandparents lived through the great depression, and until the day they died covered their furniture in plastic so that it would last longer. In their home, you always knew when somebody sat down or stood up, because it was accompanied by the crunching of plastic! My mother internalized many of the values of the depression, which manifested in her declaring any item that had received its first scratch, "ruined!" When our relatively new electric stove received its first scratch, which did not in any way affect its performance, it was "ruined." I still recall how confused those statements made me when she declared them. Did the burners no longer work? Had the oven element gone out?

Attachment to possessions very often causes us to say unkind things to the people we love the most. One of my adult children recently dropped a big bottle of red hot sauce on a white rug we have and the bottle exploded. Had I been attached to that rug, had I an expectation that it was going to last forever, I would most likely have said something to her I would have later regretted. Because I knew the rug was going to eventually have something happen to it, I was able to help her clean it up without getting upset. After all, a human being is far more precious than a rug!

In church life we see textbook evidence of attachment every time a hymnal is updated. I decided to conduct an experiment about this truth while guest preaching at a friend's church a few years ago. I began preaching about attachment and change, and told them that they were going to have a chance to practice non-attachment when their new hymnals arrived the next week. Every face in the congregation fell so much that I almost felt bad about the experiment. Of course, I told them immediately that they were keeping their hymnals, but that they should use their reaction to gain insight into their attitude around change.

On another occasion, some years before I was ordained, I was attending a church that had small weekday services in a side chapel in addition to the Sunday services. Since the services were held on Wednesdays at 9am and Fridays at 6:30am, they weren't heavily attended, but there were usually between eight and twelve worshipers in the twenty-four seat chapel. One Wednesday a new person came to the service and unwittingly sat in the seat that one of the regulars, an eighty four year old woman, usually occupied. I assumed that she would adapt, and just choose another seat when she arrived in the name of hospitality and welcoming the new person. I could not have been more wrong. She walked in, stormed up to him, and said, "You are in my seat. You will have to move." The values of this woman's spirituality could not overcome her attachment to a chair in a chapel, of all things. Needless to say, the visitor never came back!

What is the solution to attachment? The late Buddhist teacher Ajahn Chah owned a lovely tea cup from which he loved to drink his tea. When asked if he was concerned that he would become attached to the tea cup and therefore be sad when it breaks, he shared his unique outlook. He said that he was fully aware that one day the cup would break, so when he looked at the tea cup he envisioned it as already broken. In that way, he said, when the cup did break he wouldn't be sad because in his mind it would have been broken for years. Imagine if we could take that same attitude toward our new car, or our new flat screen television, or our bodies.

We are a culture obsessed with our bodies. We work out at the gym every day, train for marathons, go on the newest fad diet, watch television programs like "The Biggest Loser," hire personal trainers, have plastic surgery, inject toxins into our bodies to make our wrinkles go away, and engage in a host of other practices because we are attached to youth and believe we can avoid aging. Certainly exercise is good for us if it doesn't become an obsession, but many westerners have a real problem with moderation. When we become attached to our physical appearance or the appearance of our life partners (or both), we are in denial about the reality of life, and are setting ourselves up for disappointment. We live not in reality, not in the present moment, but in a fantasy world. We do our best to rewrap the package of our bodies, but internal signs of aging still occur. One day we will all die. Some people have said that we begin dying the day we are born. I'm not quite that cynical, but it is a view that is worth considering every now and again.

In the book of Ecclesiastes in the Bible we read that there is a time and a season for everything. Attachment, in its zeal to keep everything just the way it is, actually keeps us from growing and moving forward. The amazing truth is that living things either grow or die. There is no living thing that exists in a state of equilibrium, yet attachment is all about equilibrium. There are beautiful things about aging, as there are about youth, that we will completely miss if we are in denial about where we are on the life cycle.

If we learned to celebrate change, even the personal changes that seem to bring limitations, we could let go of our attachments and start fully engaging reality. If we started looking at our wrinkles and gray (or disappearing) hair as signs of experience and maturity instead of looking for a partner thirty years younger than us to create the illusion that we aren't really as old as the calendar tells us we are, our self esteem would actually sky rocket. Now in my fifties, I move a little slower than I used to and have had a few surgeries to repair the damage I did to my body in my twenties and thirties when I believed I was invincible, but I can honestly say that no situation could arise now that I couldn't handle gracefully - thought I don't always succed! I certainly couldn't have said that twenty five years ago. I'm not going to leave my wife and look for a new twenty year old girlfriend. What would we talk about? I'd have to listen to her music, and I'd rather have my finger nails pulled out with a pliers that listen to popular music! I can't play softball anymore, a game I loved, but I do have the satisfaction of being very good at what I do and taking on new challenges like writing this book that I couldn't have done back when I was playing a lot of softball.

We can even become attached to our understanding of God. If you get upset when you meet someone who believes differently than you, you are attached to your view of God. If someone calls you up and professes belief in the Flying Spaghetti Monster and you feel you blood pressure rise, you are attached to God. If what I wrote earlier in this book about the Virgin Mary caused you chest pains, you are attached to your religious viewpoint. Many of us might believe that we should be attached to our religious or spiritual views, but we would be wrong. Attachment is different from having strong beliefs, attachment is expecting our beliefs will never change and if they do resolving to beat them into submission. Hopefully, if we are involved in spiritual or religious practice, at the very least our understanding of our practices will deepen. That deepening is change. If we become attached, change and growth cannot possibly occur. If someone says they believe in the Flying Spaghetti Monster, that's fine for them. Holding a view of non-attachment to our own spiritual beliefs doesn't mean we change them every time a new idea comes along but it does mean that we don't allow ourselves to get upset just because another person mentions a new idea. There have been countless wars fought because people couldn't let other people believe as they did but rather felt compelled to change them. That may be spiritual attachment at it worst.

13 WHERE DO WE GO FROM HERE?

We live in a time of great transition and transformation on almost every level – personally, locally, nationally and internationally, politically, culturally, spiritually and religiously. Western Christianity in particular has reached a tipping point wherein it will either hold on to the past in a kind of self inflicted death hold or move into the future. The Latin root of our word religion means "to bind" or "tie back." It's a very apt meaning, but we need to ask ourselves if Divinity is best expressed and experienced by the entire creation continuing to be in bondage or if we will recognize what contemporary psychology recognized long ago: People need freedom to flourish. There will always be more than enough religious leaders willing to place people into bondage, but the trends indicate that fewer and fewer people are willing to allow themselves to be so bound. The long term strategy of religions that claim to have all the answers while refusing to allow any questions to be asked has run its course. We are indeed on the cusp of the next great re-formation of Christian spirituality. It is a reformation that may well see the death of Christian religion as we have known it, at least in the forms that create bondage. From its ashes something new - at the very least a new understanding of Christianity - will emerge. I believe what will emerge will be healthy spirituality, but to be healthy such a spirituality must recognize that it can't only be fed by a single tradition. The new spirituality will recognize all of the great wisdom teachers and traditions, from Jesus to Moses to Muhammad to Buddha, to Krishna and others, with each person free to examine the beliefs and teachers that resonate most with them personally. If there really is only one God, then all of the great spiritual masters have been pointing to the same God. The days of feeling a tribal need to defend our religion simply must end if we ever are to have peace on Earth.

Our resistance to such change is rooted in fear of the unknown. We don't know what our worship will look like in twenty years or if we will even call it worship. I suspect it won't look very much like worship at all, at least in that our motivation for gathering together is already changing. We know that we aren't gathering to appease an angry God, for such a God is nothing more than the product of human beings projecting their own anger onto the Divine. The reason for gathering must be to nurture our own spiritual journey. If we are going to be successful in nurturing ourselves, it only makes sense that we are going to need to use forms, messages, and music that we find nurturing in our twenty-first century world. That doesn't mean we will automatically throw away everything more than five years old, but it does mean we must be willing to try new things. Historically, the Christian Church hasn't been very good at trying new things!

In the future, our beliefs are likely to evolve, as beliefs always have. Many people resist the notion that beliefs evolve, but consider the "biblical principle" that the earth is flat. Many people expected Christopher Columbus to sail right off the edge of the Earth. Galileo was excommunicated by the Church for daring to suggest that the Earth revolved around the sun, and it took until the twentieth century for the Church to apologize and reinstate him. There is no way to predict precisely how our beliefs will change because we don't know what new information will be uncovered in the future. Our job as contemporary people is to live into the reality that we are all God bearers, inseparably connected to God and nothing we can do or say could ever change that truth. As we try on new beliefs to see if they fit we need not be afraid that the God of Love is somehow intolerant of our integrity!

Our practices will surely change, too. As someone who values the sacramental life, I recognize that we need to develop new ways of being sacramental if we have any hope of reaching those who got a case of food poisoning in the traditional Church. As someone who appreciates and loves music from Gregorian chant to contemporary popular music, honesty compels me to admit that more people love the latter than the former. What will be needed are creative people to write new music that reflects our new openness to the diversity inherent in God's vast creation. Our prayers will have to change as well to reflect our growing understanding of God. Most traditional prayer forms used in worship are still based in Atonement Theology, which says that God sacrificed Jesus to satisfy God's uncontrollable wrath. Those prayers no longer reflect our understanding of either God or Jesus, and so they must be replaced with prayers that we can say with integrity.

One of the changes we must institute now is that we must stop talking of God and Jesus as if they were some sort of cosmic superheroes waiting to descend on us and save the day. Instead, we must start living into God Consciousness, the realization that God dwells in each of us and we are capable agents of change in our lives and in our world who do not need rescuing! We need to understand the full implications of our own divinity, and recognize that when we lose sight of either our own divinity of the Divinity of others we fall into errors of perspective. The best way of accomplishing these goals is through developing a meditation or contemplative prayer practice – the terms are synonymous. Learning to spend time in the silence is the essence of growing in God Consciousness. Since God transcends language, all the talking in the world won't get us any closer to understanding God. The frustrating part of that truth can be that as we grow in God Consciousness we find that the ability of language to adequately describe our experience actually decreases, but there is comfort in knowing that we know and understand more and more as time goes on.

So again we ask, "Where do we go from here?" In the past I would have said toward union with God, but I now realize that we always have been and always will be inseparably connected to and with God and so I would today say we move toward full union with God, a state that many call enlightenment. I define enlightenment as living in full awareness of our connectedness to God – of God moving in, through, and as us – and in the full awareness that everything and everybody else is also permanently connected to God, because it is from the One we call God that everything has come forth! Enlightenment isn't something new, some sort of new realization – in fact, it is quite the opposite. Enlightenment is recalling what has always been, what Buddhists call our Buddha Nature and what I like to call our God Nature. Our God Nature gets obscured by our doubts, our struggles, and for many of us by a religious system that tries to make us something less than the God bearers we are. Our job is to polish the mirror into which we gaze, to remove the years of crud that make us seem to be something other than we are: Divinity incarnate. We polish the mirror by spending time in meditation and contemplation; in spiritual reading, practice, and discussion; and by entering into relationship with and loving one another. We polish the mirror by refusing to believe we are less than we always have been: Divine. As we polish the mirror, we come to see the answer to an old Zen Buddhist koan: "Show me the face you had before you were born." We see that face come into focus as we polish the mirror. The face we see is God looking back at us.

Lest we all run out and start polishing our mirrors with great vigor, I am reminded of the title of a very wonderful little book by Chogyam Trungpa Rinpoche, The Path is the Goal. The spiritual life is not a race. In fact, rushing through to get our mirror polished is rather counter productive. There are many lessons that must be learned along the way, and I have learned that it is precisely at the moment that people think they have "arrived" that they tend to find out just how far from their destination they really are. Even if you did manage to get your mirror completely polished tomorrow, the odds are that the day after tomorrow someone would throw a clump of mud on it and obscure your view again. I say that because all of us have moments when we lose sight of our divinity and act, react, or respond out of a belief that we somehow are lacking or deficient. Such events cause the silver frames of our mirrors to tarnish a bit, and the journey continues. The Path is not just about seeing the face of God in your mirror, it is also about being *able to continue to see that face in all the ways that life may find us.* In the words of one of my favorite philosophers, St. Steven of Aerosmith, "Life's a journey, not a destination."

Eventually, the Path leads us beyond our transition from this life as a spiritual being having a human experience back to and yet also beyond our pre-incarnate state. As a Universalist, I believe that the whole world is "saved," despite the fact that many of us don't realize the full implications of that. What happens if we transition before we have our mirrors fully polished and have lived into the truth of the divinity of all that is? Asked another way, what happens if we transition without having learned everything we have come here to learn? I believe the answer is that we come back. There have long been Christians, as well as members of Eastern religions, who believe in rebirth or reincarnation. Clearly, people of Jesus' time believed in reincarnation because they believed that it was necessary for Elijah to return before the Messiah came. I have talked to enough credible, perfectly sane people who have had memories of past lives that I can no longer discount their stories as flights of fancy. I also remember a recurring dream that I had as a very young boy of running down a narrow, crowded street and being run through on the left side of my chest with a spear. It was only years later after studying Leif Erikson in school that I recognized the furs and helmet I was wearing in my dream as those of my Scandinavian ancestors. Was that a past life memory? I honestly don't know, but I don't know that it wasn't such a memory.

Did the great despots of history learn what they came to Earth to learn before they died? Perhaps they did, but if they didn't then I have no problem with the possibility of their reincarnation.

No matter what you believe happens after we transition, we as a people need to develop a much healthier understanding of and attitude toward death. Properly understood and prepared for, our transition can be a time of great spiritual growth. Unfortunately, in Western culture, that is the exception to the rule. In my years of ministry and in my wife's years of practice as first a cardiac and now a hospice nurse, we have seen more dysfunction around death than any other life transition. From family dysfunction, to fear of the unknown, to unrealistic expectations and hopes for recovery of the terminally ill, to fights about inheritance, impending death brings out the worst in families. We must address death in our spirituality if we are to stop making those who are preparing to transition the victims of their survivors!

Finally, we desperately need to develop a healthy sexual ethic. We need to move away from puritanical nonsense and into an honest discussion of our sexuality. We need to stop seeing sexuality, which is a very natural process by which each and every one of us came to be on this planet and through which relationships deepen in their intimacy, as if it were some kind of problem to be avoided if at all possible. Can we learn to see that sexuality is an event in which two God bearers come to share in each other's divinity? Can we acknowledge that it is in and through orgasm that humans experience a foretaste of our return to living as purely spiritual (not embodied) beings? Can we see that if God is the energy behind the creation and continuation of everything that is, God is present in sexuality as well? Is it possible for us to realize that humans are all sexual beings and that is a normal state for us? The answer to all of these questions must be, "YES!" if we are to move beyond the sexual dysfunction that is rampant in our culture.

Of course, if we look at all that is to be done it can seem a bit overwhelming. My experience of the past several years has taught me that when the time is right change will occur. Our job is to live into our divinity on a daily basis and encourage others to do the same. As we do so, and as we spread the truly Good News that we are all inseparably connected to divinity because we are all God bearers, I believe we will transform the world one person at a time. The rest will take care of itself!

ABOUT THE AUTHOR

Bishop Craig Bergland was born and raised in the Milwaukee, Wisconsin area. He attended Marquette University and completed Bachelor of Arts degrees in both Theology and Psychology at Wisconsin Lutheran College. He did graduate work in Religious Studies at Cardinal Stritch University and earned a Master of Divinity Degree and Doctor of Divinity from the Anglican Divinity School.

Craig was ordained in 1999 at Community of the Living Spirit, an ecumenical faith community in suburban Milwaukee. In 2004 he was elected Presiding Bishop of the Universal Anglican Church. Having a passion for the full inclusion of all people in the life of the Church, Craig has been active in The Bishops and Elders Council, HRC's Clergy Call for Justice, and has been a leader in religious outreach at Milwaukee's Pridefest celebration. Craig has written <u>Rite III</u>, an inclusive language worship book that includes an inclusive language version of the Psalter.

In addition to his ongoing role as Presiding Bishop of the Universal Anglican Church, Bishop Bergland's current project is Christ Enlight Interspirituality, a system of Interspirituality that recognizes Jesus as primarily a wisdom and enlightenment teacher. Christ Enlight Interspirituality seeks to journey with all people from all spiritual backgrounds and perspectives, and affirms all people as bearing the very DNA of God, from whom they can never be separated. An outreach of Christ Enlight Interspirituality, Compassionate Heart Gatherings are spiritual gatherings of those seeking spiritual tools to transform themselves, their communities, and the world. Craig's website is BishopCraig.com, where he blogs regularly.

He lives in Milwaukee, Wisconsin with his wife Erin; their adult children Peter, Tori, and Brandie; and their grandchildren Natalia and Greyson.

Made in the USA
Middletown, DE
20 May 2021

40110019R00116